What Marketers Can Learn from Martial Arts

THE PATH TO MASTERY AND MARKET DOMINANCE

What Marketers Can Learn from Martial Arts

THE PATH TO MASTERY AND MARKET DOMINANCE

Subba Rao Chaganti

BSP **BS Publications**®
An Imprint of **BSP Books Pvt. Ltd.**
4-4-309/316, Giriraj Lane,
Sultan Bazar, Hyderabad - 500 001,
Telangana, India.

What Marketers can Learn from Martial Arts: The Path to Mastery and Market Dominance

by Subba Rao Chaganti

Published by:

BSP BS Publications®

An Imprint of **BSP Books Pvt. Ltd.**

4-4-309/316, Giriraj Lane, Sultan Bazar,
Hyderabad - 500 001, Telangana, India.
Phone : 040 - 23445688
e-mail : info@bspbooks.net
www.bspbooks.net

ISBN: 978-93-47311-32-1 (Hardback)

Disclaimer

This book is an independent work of educational commentary, strategic analysis, and philosophical interpretation. The ideas, frameworks, comparisons, and observations presented herein are intended solely for learning, discussion, and professional development purposes.

References to martial arts philosophies, disciplines, practices, principles, traditions, concepts, terminology, historical figures, public personalities, organizations, brands, products, campaigns, and companies are made exclusively for purposes of commentary, criticism, education, illustration, analysis, and comparative discussion.

All trademarks, service marks, trade names, logos, slogans, brand identities, and registered marks mentioned in this book remain the property of their respective owners. Their inclusion does not imply endorsement, sponsorship, affiliation, partnership, authorization, or approval of this work by any individual, company, organization, federation, or rights holder.

Any references to advertising campaigns, public business strategies, public interviews, public statements, or publicly known case studies are based on information believed to be publicly available and reasonably accurate at the time of writing. The author makes no claim of ownership over any referenced brand names, campaigns, or corporate materials.

The martial arts principles discussed in this book are interpreted conceptually and metaphorically for applications in business, leadership, branding, strategy, communication, discipline, and personal mastery. This book is not intended to serve as formal instruction, certification, training guidance, or authoritative representation of any martial art, dojo, lineage, federation, school, or combat system.

Any brief quotations or attributed statements included in this work are used in accordance with principles of commentary, scholarship, educational discussion, and fair analytical reference. Every effort has been made to avoid unauthorized reproduction of copyrighted material. If any copyright holder believes material has been used improperly, the publisher and author invite communication for prompt review and resolution.

The opinions, interpretations, frameworks, and conclusions expressed in this book are solely those of the author and do not necessarily reflect the views of any referenced company, organization, institution, practitioner, athete, or public figure.

This work is provided for informational and educational purposes only. The author and publisher disclaim responsibility for any business, financial, strategic, commercial, personal, organizational, or professional decisions made based on the contents of this book. Readers are encouraged to exercise independent judgment and seek professional advice where appropriate.

AI Transparency Note

Portions of the research, structuring, drafting assistance, ideation, and editorial development process for this book involved the responsible use of AI-assisted tools under the author's direction, supervision, and editorial judgment. All final interpretations, analyses, conclusions, selections, and written content were reviewed, curated, and approved by the author, who assumes full responsibility for the finished work.

Acknowledgements

No book is ever written alone, and this one — bridging the worlds of marketing, psychology, and martial philosophy — has drawn strength from many teachers, collaborators, and companions on the path.

My deepest gratitude goes first to Anil Shah, publisher, and Nikunjesh Shah, whose belief in unconventional ideas has continually inspired me to explore new frontiers of thought. Their encouragement to connect marketing with diverse disciplines has made this book possible. I also extend my appreciation to Naresh Davergave and his design team at PharmaMed Press, whose precision, patience, and creative integrity ensured that every page reflected the spirit of mastery this book seeks to convey.

I owe a special debt to my family — my wife Mahalakshmi, my children Srinivasa Phanindra, Geetha, Lavanya, Satya Sankara Aditya, Sowmya, and Chaitanya, and my grandchildren Aditi, Eesha, Surya, and Shriya — for their unwavering love, understanding, and quiet support during long writing sessions and countless revisions. Their patience has been my anchor, and their faith has been my motivation.

I also wish to thank the martial arts practitioners, teachers, and writers whose philosophies form the heartbeat of this work — Bruce Lee, Gichin Funakoshi, Morihei Ueshiba, Miyamoto Musashi, and Jigoro Kano — whose words and wisdom have transcended the dojo to illuminate life, leadership, and creativity. Although centuries apart, their lessons on discipline, humility, and awareness resonate with the challenges marketers face in mastering their craft today.

To my friends and colleagues in the pharmaceutical and marketing community, thank you for the countless conversations, debates, and reflections that shaped this book. Many of you shared stories of campaigns, teams, and transformations that mirrored the very spirit of martial training — repetition, adaptation, and resilience. Your experiences gave theory its living form.

I also acknowledge the profound influence of psychologists, behavioral scientists, and strategists — from Daniel Kahneman to Mihaly Csikszentmihalyi, Carol Dweck, and Angela Duckworth — whose research bridges the scientific and the spiritual. Their work has made it possible to speak of mastery not as mysticism but as measurable progress.

Finally, I wish to thank my readers and students — those who constantly challenge the known, question the familiar, and strive to understand marketing as an evolving human art. Your curiosity is the real dojo; your pursuit of learning is what keeps this discipline alive.

Like every martial arts enthusiast, I stand on the shoulders of those who trained before me. Whatever wisdom this book contains belongs to them; whatever its shortcomings are, they are mine alone.

With deep gratitude,

Subba Rao Chaganti

Preface

Every great discipline — whether it's swordsmanship, painting, or marketing — begins with a paradox: mastery is not about control, but about awareness.

When I first began exploring the relationship between marketing and martial arts, it seemed almost whimsical — one concerned with combat, the other with commerce. But the deeper I studied both, the more I recognized an uncanny symmetry. Beneath their surface differences lies a shared code of discipline, humility, adaptability, and respect. Both are, at their essence, lifelong paths of self-cultivation.

Martial arts are not merely about fighting; they are about seeing. The seasoned martial artist learns to read motion, intention, rhythm — to anticipate rather than react. The skilled marketer does the same. Behind every successful campaign lies a sensitivity to timing, context, and energy — the pulse of culture, the heartbeat of the consumer. Just as a black belt knows that strength without timing is wasted, the marketer learns that creativity without empathy is noise.

In dojo halls across centuries, students learned through repetition, reflection, and respect — the same process that underpins the world's most enduring brands. The kata, or formalized patterns of practice, mirror the structured creativity that great marketers use to refine campaigns. The sensei, or mentor, represents what every effective leader must be: a custodian of wisdom and integrity. And the belt system—white to black—is not a ranking of dominance but a reminder that every master remains an eternal student.

This book was written to explore that shared journey — to bridge two worlds that, at first glance, could not be more different yet, in practice, follow identical principles. Each chapter connects martial concepts to marketing realities: discipline to execution, adaptability to innovation, humility to brand ethics, and flow to creativity. The goal is not to romanticize either art, but to distill the timeless lessons that unite them.

In an era where algorithms dominate and attention is currency, it's easy to forget that marketing, like martial arts, is fundamentally human. Technology can amplify skill, but it cannot replace character. The marketer who approaches their craft with the discipline of a martial artist — who trains daily, learns continuously, and respects both competitor and consumer — will find that mastery is not a myth but a method.

As you read, you'll encounter not just theories but stories — of Bruce Lee's fluid philosophy, of brands like Nike and Patagonia that embody purpose and restraint, of campaigns that succeeded through humility rather than hype. Each serves as a reminder that the true path to mastery is not about fighting harder but about seeing more clearly.

The martial artist bows before entering the dojo — a gesture of respect for the practice ahead. In the same spirit, I invite you to enter these pages with openness and curiosity. What follows is not a manual of tactics, but a meditation on mastery — the art of awareness in motion.

Subba Rao Chaganti

Contents

Introduction

Why Compare Marketing and Martial Arts?

On the surface, marketing and martial arts have little in common. One is a domain of boardrooms, data dashboards, and digital ads; the other, of dojos, discipline, and deliberate movement. Yet when you strip both down to their essence—focus, adaptability, timing, and mastery—you begin to see a remarkable symmetry. Both are about understanding an opponent, reading the environment, anticipating moves, and responding with precision. Both reward patience, self-awareness, and practice over impulse and luck.

When Bruce Lee told his students to "be like water," he wasn't speaking just to fighters—he was revealing a universal strategy: adapt to circumstance without losing form. In marketing, the same principle applies. Brands that cling rigidly to old tactics perish; those that adapt fluidly—like Apple reinventing its narrative from computers to creativity, or Nike turning athletes into archetypes—endure and dominate. In fact, marketing scholars like Philip Kotler have long framed marketing not as manipulation but as value exchange and relationship building—a philosophy not unlike the respect and reciprocity that define traditional martial arts.

The Shared Psychology of Mastery

Psychologists such as Anders Ericsson have shown that expertise, whether in chess, music, or martial arts, comes not from talent but from deliberate practice: hours of focused, feedback-driven effort that pushes boundaries. Marketing, too, rewards this kind of disciplined refinement. Campaigns that win hearts and shape behavior are not spontaneous flashes of genius—they are the result of constant testing, measurement, and iteration. The A/B test is a marketer's kata, a ritualized pattern repeated until mastery is achieved.

The journey from white belt to black belt mirrors the marketer's evolution from novice to strategist. The early practitioner mimics others, follows scripts, and obeys rules. The advanced one internalizes principles, adapts fluidly, and teaches others. In both, mastery is never static—it's a continuous loop of learning, humility, and reinvention.

Competition and the Code of Conduct

Martial artists live by codes—the dojo kun, bushidō, or tao—emphasizing respect, honor, and restraint. Marketing, though competitive, is similarly governed by ethical frameworks. The best marketers don't aim to defeat competitors but to serve customers better. This mirrors the martial artist's creed: victory without honor is hollow.

When Red Bull staged "Stratos," the live-streamed space jump, it wasn't an act of aggression toward rivals—it was an expression of philosophy: courage, human potential, and the thrill of limits. It turned marketing into a martial performance—disciplined, daring, and precise.

Strategy, Adaptability, and the Art of Reading Opponents

In martial arts, reading an opponent's intent—subtle shifts in balance, gaze, or breathing—can determine the outcome before a punch is thrown. In marketing, the equivalent lies in reading data, sentiment, and shifting consumer desires. Netflix's algorithmic agility, or Spotify's micro-segmentation, resembles a martial artist's instinctive adjustment mid-fight: sensing, reacting, and redirecting momentum.

Even Sun Tzu's The Art of War, a text often cited by both generals and executives, teaches that "to know the enemy and know yourself" ensures success in a hundred battles. Replace "enemy" with "market" and "battle" with "campaign," and the timelessness of that advice becomes evident.

The Philosophy Behind the Practice

Every martial art—from Aikido's harmony to Brazilian Jiu-Jitsu's leverage—embodies a philosophy that transcends combat. Likewise, great marketing transcends selling. It's storytelling with purpose, empathy in action, and alignment between what's promised and delivered. Both demand an understanding of human nature.

Miyamoto Musashi, the 17th-century samurai and author of The Book of Five Rings, wrote that "the ultimate aim of martial arts is not having to use them." For marketers, the ultimate aim may be similar: building brands so authentic and trusted that persuasion becomes unnecessary.

The Path to Mastery and Market Dominance

The world's most enduring brands—like the most legendary martial artists—embody mastery as a mindset, not a milestone. They practice vigilance, evolve with change, and see failure as feedback, not defeat. Both marketing and martial arts demand resilience—the kind forged through repetition, reflection, and respect for the process.

Comparing marketing to martial arts is not a gimmick; it is a recognition of a deeper truth about how excellence is achieved in any field. The dojo and the boardroom share a sacred law: mastery is not about winning once—it's about never ceasing to improve.

The Surprising Parallels: An Overview

When you first place a marketer beside a martial artist, the connection seems improbable. One studies consumer psychology, while the other focuses on body mechanics and combat flow. Yet the deeper you look, the more you begin to see a shared DNA — a pattern of mastery that transcends the medium. Both disciplines revolve around the same invisible axis: awareness, adaptability, and alignment.

In martial arts, awareness is physical — the feel of balance, timing, and distance. In marketing, it's psychological — the pulse of the audience, the rhythm of the market, the moment when emotion meets message. In both, awareness precedes action. A fighter who throws a punch without reading the opponent wastes energy; a marketer who launches a campaign without understanding the audience wastes budget. The battlefield and the marketplace may differ, but the principle is the same: perception before persuasion.

The Training Mindset: From the Dojo to the Boardroom

Walk into a traditional dojo, and you'll find students bowing before practice — not to an instructor, but to the spirit of learning itself. This ritual humility is at the heart of every craft that values improvement over ego. The best marketers share this same ethos. They test, iterate, fail, and refine. They respect the process, not just the outcome.

Modern behavioral science backs this up. Studies by Stanford psychologist Carol Dweck on growth mindset reveal that those who see skill as something to develop — rather than a fixed talent — achieve more sustained success. This mindset can be easily drawn from martial traditions, where every mistake is a teacher and every repetition a path to refinement. The lesson is universal: mastery is cumulative, not instantaneous.

The Art of Adaptation

Every martial art is born from adaptation. Judo turned opponents 'strength into leverage; Jeet Kune Do dismantled rigidity itself. Marketing, too, is an art of adaptation — adjusting strategy in response to shifting markets, technologies, and cultural moods. When Coca-Cola rebranded "Share a Coke," replacing its logo with common names, it didn't just sell soda — it adapted to an era of personalization and self-expression.

Bruce Lee's idea of formless form — of using no way as way — is echoed in the agility of modern marketing teams who pivot campaigns mid-launch based on real-time analytics. In both fields, success belongs to those who sense change before it's obvious, and who act before others react.

Strategy and Flow

In both disciplines, the most effective strategies are often invisible. A martial artist doesn't fight harder; they fight smarter, flowing around resistance rather than through it. Likewise, master marketers don't push products — they guide audiences effortlessly toward belief and desire. Mihaly Csikszentmihalyi's research on flow states describes it as a state of total immersion, in which skill and challenge balance perfectly. The martial artist finds it in the fight; the marketer finds it in creative alignment — when insight, message, and timing strike in unison.

Steve Jobs once said that simplicity is the ultimate sophistication. That could have come straight from a Zen dojo. The highest form of both arts is not complexity but clarity — the clean, precise motion that hides decades of discipline.

Respect, Resilience, and Responsibility

The most powerful parallel of all may be moral, not strategic. Both marketing and martial arts carry immense influence — one over behavior, the other over force. With power comes the burden of restraint. The martial artist's code forbids misuse; the ethical marketer's code warns against manipulation. Both understand that mastery without integrity corrodes from within.

Resilience, too, binds them. Every fighter who's been knocked down knows that the lesson lies not in the fall but in the rise. Every marketer who's seen a failed campaign knows the same truth. In martial arts, scars are signs of learning; in marketing, so are metrics.

A Universal Path to Mastery

The surprising parallels between these worlds remind us that mastery in any field follows a similar trajectory: awareness, discipline, humility, adaptability, and integrity. Whether wielding a sword or a strategy, the journey is inward first — toward self-control, self-knowledge, and balance.

Marketing, at its best, is not a battle for attention but a dialogue of respect — a meeting of needs and narratives. Martial arts, at their best, are not about defeating others but about conquering the self. In that shared pursuit lies the true bridge between the dojo and the digital marketplace: both are arenas where excellence is earned, not claimed.

Section 1

Foundations

Definitions: What is Marketing? What is Martial Arts?

To understand the parallel, we must begin with clarity. Marketing, at its core, is the discipline of creating, communicating, and delivering value to satisfy human needs profitably. But that definition, drawn from the American Marketing Association, only scratches the surface. Behind every campaign lies an attempt to understand behavior — to decode what drives people to act, believe, or belong. In that sense, marketing is not just about persuasion; it's about empathy, psychology, and timing.

Martial arts, too, are often misinterpreted as systems of combat. Historically, however, they emerged as philosophies of self-mastery rather than domination. The Japanese term *Budo* literally means "the way of stopping conflict." The Chinese wushu translates to "skill through discipline." From kung fu to karate-do, every tradition shares the same premise: the fight is merely a metaphor — the real opponent is within.

In both realms, technique is only the outer shell. The true mastery lies in mindset. The marketer studies consumers not to manipulate, but to understand their world; the martial artist trains the body not to overpower, but to harmonize with circumstance. Both become, in their own way, students of human nature.

Core Objectives: Value Creation vs. Self-Improvement

At first glance, the goals diverge. Marketing aims at value creation—aligning a product's promise with a customer's needs. Martial arts aim at self-improvement — aligning intention with action, body with mind. Yet these objectives mirror each other more closely than they seem.

Consider the customer journey, a term modern marketers use to map the stages of awareness, interest, engagement, and loyalty. Each stage demands patience and precision — much like a martial artist advancing through the belt system. The marketer's journey toward resonance mirrors the fighter's path toward flow. In both, there is no shortcut. Every step matters.

The martial artist polishes the same move thousands of times until it becomes effortless. The marketer refines a message through countless iterations until it connects seamlessly. Both disciplines demand respect for process over outcome — the kind of diligence psychologist Mihaly Csikszentmihalyi identified as the foundation of creative mastery.

Historical Evolution: From Ancient Dojo to Modern Campaigns

The dojo, centuries ago, was not just a training hall but a sanctuary of learning. Here, farmers, monks, and samurai practiced forms that cultivated not only strength but serenity. Martial arts evolved through observation of movement, rhythm, and the natural world. The principle of kaizen (continuous improvement) was born in this setting long before it became a management buzzword in postwar Japan.

Marketing, too, has undergone its own evolution. In the early 20th century, it was transactional — about selling what was made. By the mid-century, thinkers like Peter Drucker reframed it as understanding the customer so well that the product fits them and sells itself. Then came Philip Kotler, who infused marketing with a moral dimension — turning it from persuasion into service.

The modern marketing dojo is digital. The practitioners are armed not with swords but with data, social listening tools, and storytelling frameworks. Yet, the spirit remains ancient: observe, adapt, and master the self before mastering the opponent. The algorithm has replaced the sparring partner, but the challenge — timing, rhythm, and responsiveness — remains the same.

Bridging Two Traditions of Mastery

Both marketing and martial arts belong to lineages that prize discipline over dominance. The marketer who understands audiences better than anyone else wins not because they shout louder but because they listen deeper. The martial artist who triumphs does so not through aggression but through timing, patience, and control.

Each discipline teaches that mastery is not a state but a path. In martial arts, the black belt signifies not the end but the beginning of true learning. In marketing, success — whether a viral campaign or a record quarter — only opens new questions: How can we do better? How can we remain relevant?

The foundation of both arts is humility in the face of complexity. And perhaps that is the ultimate common ground: both marketer and martial artist learn that power without purpose is empty — and mastery without meaning, hollow.

Section 2

Core Similarities

The Apprentice-to-Master Model: Learning from Mentors

Every discipline has its lineage — a chain of transmission through which knowledge deepens, evolves, and endures. In martial arts, this is literal: each student traces their heritage through a sensei, who learned from another master, who in turn was shaped by yet another before them. Skill and philosophy are passed not through lectures but through repetition, observation, and lived example.

Marketing, though often portrayed as a fast-moving, self-taught field, follows the same pattern in spirit. Behind every legendary campaign, there is a lineage — a mentor who taught the art of positioning, a strategist who showed how to "listen between the lines," a leader who modeled integrity under pressure. The marketing dojo may be the agency floor, the brand war room, or even the online classroom, but the principle remains: mastery is relational.

Anders Ericsson's landmark studies on deliberate practice showed that mentorship accelerates skill development not because the teacher provides shortcuts, but because they guide attention — helping the student see what matters. In martial arts, the master corrects the stance by a few degrees; in marketing, the mentor refines the insight by a few words. Both corrections can change the entire trajectory of performance.

Discipline, Routine, and Practice

If martial arts can be reduced to one word, it might be discipline. Hours of forms, breath control, drills — not glamorous, often tedious, yet utterly transformative. Each repetition engrains not just movement but mindset. The student learns that excellence is born not of intensity but of consistency.

In marketing, the same law applies. Campaigns that appear to go viral effortlessly are usually the product of relentless iteration—brainstorming, testing, refining, and testing again. Data analysts sift through thousands of metrics much like martial artists repeat thousands of strikes: not for spectacle, but for subtlety.

Behavioral research backs this parallel. Psychologist B.F. Skinner's work on operant conditioning revealed how repetition reinforces desired behaviors, while Charles Duhigg's studies in *The Power of Habit* show how routine underpins sustained success. The marketer's calendar of daily analytics reviews and campaign stand-ups is, in a sense, a kata — a ritual of refinement that turns chaos into rhythm.

Discipline, in both worlds, is less about constraint than liberation. The martial artist practices control to achieve freedom of movement; the marketer practices structure to achieve freedom of creativity. What looks rigid from the outside is, in truth, the scaffolding of flow.

The Importance of Specialization (and its Limits)

Every martial artist begins with a style — Shotokan, Taekwondo, BJJ — each with its philosophy and focus. But as mastery grows, the practitioner learns to see beyond form. Bruce Lee's Jeet Kune Do broke away from traditional rigidity with a radical insight: "Absorb what is useful, discard what is not."

Marketers, too, begin in silos — product management, digital strategy, copywriting, analytics. Yet, the best rise above their discipline to integrate them. The great brand strategist must know how creative storytelling merges with behavioral economics; the digital marketer must sense when data insights must yield to intuition.

In both martial arts and marketing, specialization is a stage — not a destination. It gives structure early on, but becomes a cage if held too long. A marketer who clings to one channel or one formula risks obsolescence, just as a martial artist who refuses to evolve loses touch with living practice. The highest mastery lies in synthesis — the ability to integrate and flow across domains.

Adaptability: The "Be Like Water" Philosophy

In 1971, Bruce Lee appeared on The Pierre Berton Show and spoke words that would ripple through decades: "Empty your mind. Be formless, shapeless, like water." He was describing the pinnacle of martial adaptability — a state where one flows with the opponent, reshaping one's tactics without losing center.

In marketing, adaptability is equally vital. Consumer attention shifts faster than ever; what resonated yesterday feels stale today. A pandemic rewrites buying behaviors overnight. A single tweet can reshape a brand narrative in hours. In such turbulence, rigidity is ruinous.

The marketers who thrive — think of Oreo's spontaneous "You can still dunk in the dark" tweet during the 2013 Super Bowl blackout — embody this water-like flexibility. They prepare meticulously but stay open to improvisation. Data informs their instinct, but instinct guides their timing.

Cognitive flexibility research in neuroscience supports this: adaptability enhances creative problem-solving by engaging the prefrontal cortex — the same region activated in athletes performing under pressure. Whether dodging a kick or managing a PR crisis, the art lies in staying calm enough to sense opportunity within chaos.

Competition: Navigating Rivals on the Mat and in the Market

Both marketing and martial arts are arenas of competition — but the wisest practitioners see competition not as conflict, but as context. A sparring partner reveals your blind spots; a rival brand exposes your weaknesses. In this way, competition becomes a form of collaboration — a shared pursuit of higher standards.

In the 1980s, Pepsi's Challenge campaign prompted Coca-Cola to reassess its identity, ultimately leading to "New Coke," a product that paradoxically enhanced the brand's long-term authenticity. It was a duel that taught humility — much like a match lost on the mat that awakens deeper discipline.

Martial artists speak of randori — free sparring — as a crucible of learning. Marketers engage in their own form of randori through A/B tests, market experiments, and competitive benchmarking. Both know that every encounter is feedback. Losing a round isn't failure; refusing to learn from it is.

Integrity and Ethics in Both Worlds

In traditional martial arts, a fighter's strength without integrity is dishonor. Codes such as Bushidō and the Dojo Kun remind practitioners that the ultimate aim is harmony, not harm. Marketing, when practiced ethically, operates under a similar covenant. Transparency, respect for consumer autonomy, and truth in communication are its moral equivalents of Bushidō.

When brands exploit fear or falsify promises, they break this code — and the backlash is swift. The fall of Cambridge Analytica's data manipulation in political campaigns echoes the martial warning: power misused invites defeat. Conversely, brands that align purpose with authenticity — like Patagonia or Dove's "Real Beauty" campaign — demonstrate how ethical discipline yields enduring loyalty.

Integrity, in both arts, is not ornamental; it's structural. It sustains credibility, ensures continuity, and turns skill into wisdom.

The Essence of the Parallel

What ties these parallels together is not metaphor but method. Both martial arts and marketing operate on a paradox: the more one disciplines the self, the freer one becomes. The novice focuses on moves; the master, on meaning. The marketer studies metrics; the brand visionary senses momentum. In both, the difference between a fighter and a master — or between a promoter and a storyteller — lies in awareness, humility, and the courage to evolve.

Section 3

Key Differences

Physical vs. Psychological Engagement

If martial arts are the choreography of movement, marketing is the choreography of meaning. The martial artist manipulates space, timing, and balance; the marketer manipulates attention, perception, and desire. Both are performances, but on very different stages.

The martial artist's battleground is tangible — a mat, a ring, an opponent's body. The marketer's is abstract — the human mind, filtered through screens, stories, and social influence. Neuroscientists have shown that physical mastery activates the motor cortex and cerebellum, regions tied to coordination and muscle memory. Marketing mastery, by contrast, engages the prefrontal cortex and limbic system — the centers of emotion, empathy, and decision-making.

Yet the divide is not absolute. Mirror neuron research from the University of Parma revealed that watching an action can activate the same neural pathways as performing it. This means that when a consumer feels inspired, moved, or thrilled by an ad, their body partially mirrors that emotion — a phenomenon martial artists have exploited for centuries through the poise and presence of their movements. Marketing, at its highest level, evokes this same embodied reaction — the shiver of recognition, the spark of belonging.

So while martial arts engage muscles and reflexes, and marketing engages cognition and emotion, both seek mastery of the same frontier: human behavior.

Outcomes: Victory, Survival, or Consumer Loyalty?

In martial arts, the outcome is often immediate — a strike lands, a throw succeeds, a contest ends. In marketing, results unfold over time, measured not in seconds but in sentiments. Victory in the dojo is visible; victory in the marketplace is invisible, spread across perception, memory, and choice.

The martial artist's reward is survival or triumph; the marketer's is trust and loyalty. Yet both outcomes require anticipation. A fighter anticipates an opponent's next move; a marketer anticipates a consumer's next need. Both must be attuned to subtle cues — hesitation before a strike, hesitation before a purchase.

This difference in temporal rhythm has strategic consequences. Martial arts thrive on precision in the moment; marketing thrives on consistency across time. The martial artist wins a match by reading the instant; the marketer wins the market by reading the decade. One is tactical mastery, the other strategic endurance — but both rely on awareness, timing, and discipline.

Individual Versus Team Dynamics

Martial arts, by tradition, center on the individual — the lone practitioner seeking personal mastery. Marketing, by contrast, is irreducibly collective. A successful campaign depends on collaboration among strategists, designers, analysts, storytellers, and leaders.

Yet, paradoxically, both demand selflessness. The martial artist must surrender ego to the form; the marketer must dissolve individual creativity into the shared voice of the brand. In martial arts, the kata — a solo form — only makes sense when performed with mindful awareness of imaginary opponents. In marketing, a single creative idea has meaning only when it is aligned with consumer context and cultural narrative.

Organizational psychology research from MIT's Human Dynamics Lab found that high-performing teams operate like martial ensembles: coordination depends less on hierarchy and more on rhythm — short, frequent, high-energy exchanges that build trust and intuition. The marketing dojo, it turns out, is also a chorus — every movement connected to the whole.

Short-Term Tactics vs. Long-Term Brand Building

In martial arts, the fight is ephemeral; mastery is eternal. In marketing, the campaign is transient; the brand is enduring. The difference between tactics and strategy — between the quick jab and the patient stance — defines both disciplines.

Short-term tactics in marketing — discounts, flash campaigns, viral stunts — are like sparring drills: they sharpen reflexes but don't define legacy. Long-term brand building, on the other hand, resembles the philosophy behind the martial journey — an accumulation of values, identity, and story that endures beyond individual moves.

The martial artist's belt signifies progression, not perfection. The marketer's brand equity does the same. Each new campaign adds to an invisible lineage, shaping how the audience perceives strength, trust, and purpose.

Academic studies by Les Binet and Peter Field at the IPA (Institute of Practitioners in Advertising) confirm this: short-term sales activations deliver immediate spikes, but long-term brand-building campaigns deliver sustained growth and resilience. The martial artist trains for decades to be prepared for a single decisive moment; the marketer builds trust over years to earn a single decisive choice.

The Balance between Action and Awareness

In both worlds, the most dangerous misconception is mistaking motion for progress. A flurry of punches that never lands; a flurry of posts that never resonate. The martial artist learns restraint — to move only when movement matters. The marketer, too, learns the same lesson: not every trend deserves pursuit, not every metric defines meaning.

The great divide between martial arts and marketing is therefore not philosophical, but perceptual. One seeks mastery of the outer world, the other of the inner. Yet both converge on a single truth: to master the external, one must first master the internal — the mind that chooses when to strike, and when to wait.

Section 4

Martial Arts Principles for Marketers

The "Dojo Mindset": Continuous Self-Improvement

Step inside any traditional dojo, and you immediately sense the paradox of mastery: the closer one comes to perfection, the farther it seems to recede. The walls may be bare, the air silent except for the rhythmic sound of strikes meeting pads. There are no trophies here—only the ritual of daily practice. Progress is measured not by applause, but by awareness.

In this humility lies the first great principle marketers can borrow from martial arts—the Dojo Mindset. It is the belief that learning never stops. Every campaign, every launch, every interaction is another kata—another repetition in the pursuit of excellence.

Modern research in performance psychology supports what ancient masters long knew: expertise is not linear, but cyclical. Anders Ericsson's work on deliberate practice shows that mastery depends less on raw talent and more on sustained, feedback-driven effort. Similarly, Carol Dweck's studies on growth mindset reveal that those who view skill as malleable rather than fixed outperform their peers in complex, changing environments.

The marketer's dojo is not a physical space but a mental one—an environment of curiosity, iteration, and respect for process. In companies like Google and HubSpot, "post-mortem" reviews after every campaign function like martial reflections after sparring sessions. The goal is not to blame but to understand. Just as the martial artist studies each move for balance and intent, the marketer studies each data point for insight and resonance.

The dojo mindset is less about victory and more about vigilance—a quiet, daily vow: I will be better than I was yesterday.

Tactical Adaptation: Reading the Opponent or Market

In combat, reading your opponent is everything. A flicker of hesitation, a shift in stance, a tightening of the shoulder—all reveal intent. A good martial artist doesn't react; they anticipate. They sense momentum before it becomes motion.

Marketers face an equally dynamic opponent: the market itself. Consumer sentiment shifts like footwork—subtle, continuous, often invisible until too late. The art lies not in chasing trends but in perceiving the underlying energy that drives them.

This is why companies that survive disruption often behave like seasoned fighters. Netflix, for example, saw the shift from DVDs to streaming not as a threat but as an opening—reading the industry's posture before the blow. Similarly, Nike's "Just Do It" campaign in the late 1980s wasn't just an ad; it was a counter-strike against complacency, reframing personal fitness as a universal challenge rather than an elite pursuit.

Behavioral economists like Daniel Kahneman and Richard Thaler have shown that human decisions are shaped more by context and emotion than by logic. The marketer, like the martial artist, learns to read those emotional cues—the fear before commitment, the hesitation before purchase—and to respond with empathy, not aggression.

In the dojo, the wise fighter never meets force with force. They redirect it. In the marketplace, the wise brand never confronts consumer resistance head-on. It listens, adapts, and repositions—turning friction into flow.

Mastery of Fundamentals: Campaign Basics and Kata

Every martial art begins with fundamentals—stances, blocks, and strikes—rehearsed endlessly until they become instinctual. The Japanese term kata literally means "form," but it signifies much more: a framework for discipline and creativity. Within repetition lies revelation.

Marketers, too, have their kata—the timeless principles of clarity, consistency, and connection. Long before AI-driven analytics and neuro-targeting, the fundamentals remained: understand your audience, articulate your message, and deliver value.

When Unilever's "Dirt is Good" campaign redefined the meaning of cleanliness, it wasn't a technological leap—it was a return to fundamentals: a universal insight about parenthood, freedom, and play. The execution was creative, but the foundation was human truth.

Neuroscience supports this approach. Studies from Harvard Business School demonstrate that simplicity and familiarity improve message retention by lowering cognitive load. The marketer who masters the basics—like the martial artist perfecting a single punch—achieves precision that technology alone cannot replicate.

Kata is not repetition for its own sake. It is ritualized refinement. Every email, every tagline, every pitch becomes an opportunity to align motion with meaning—until mastery looks effortless, though it never is.

The Role of Repetition: Drills and A/B Testing

In a dojo, repetition is both meditation and muscle memory. The same punch thrown ten thousand times is not the same—it evolves with awareness. Each iteration brings the practitioner closer to the flow state, where action and intention merge seamlessly.

In marketing, repetition takes the form of A/B testing, campaign optimization, and data analysis. The marketer experiments, measures, refines—over and over again. A headline tested a hundred ways is no different from a roundhouse practiced a thousand. Both seek the same goal: precision that persuades without wasted motion.

Digital marketers now live in an era of measurable refinement. Behavioral data, click-through rates, and user heatmaps serve as the sparring feedback loops of modern campaigns. The process may appear mechanical, but its essence is deeply human—an ongoing dialogue between creativity and feedback, intuition and evidence.

Repetition, as martial masters say, is not the mother of boredom but the father of excellence.

Harnessing Flow States: Focus and Presence

When a martial artist enters combat, time seems to bend. Movements blur into intuition; the mind empties of fear and fills with rhythm. Psychologist Mihaly Csikszentmihalyi referred to this as the flow state—the point where skill and challenge align so perfectly that self-consciousness disappears.

Marketers know this experience, too, though their battles take place on digital rather than physical terrain. The strategist lost in crafting a brand narrative, the designer immersed in a campaign's visual poetry, the analyst discovering patterns at 2 a.m.—all are practicing their art in a state of flow.

Research shows that teams in flow are up to five times more productive and significantly more creative. Like sparring partners synchronized in motion, marketing teams in flow communicate seamlessly, their energy converging toward shared purpose.

Martial masters cultivate flow through breath control and mindfulness; marketers cultivate it through focus and feedback. Both discover that presence—not speed—is the real secret to performance. In both arenas, distraction is defeat.

The Common Thread

The martial artist and the marketer share a covenant of craft. Both practice in cycles—study, apply, reflect, refine. Both know that mastery is not about dominating the opponent but mastering oneself: one's ego, impulses, and distractions.

In the end, the greatest campaigns, like the greatest kata, are expressions of disciplined grace. They appear effortless because every motion behind them has been practiced, tested, and perfected until art and science are indistinguishable.

Section 5

Strategy and Tactics

Building Resilience: Handling Setbacks and Failures

Every martial artist learns early that falling is part of the journey. The mat is both teacher and test. Each fall teaches balance, each bruise endurance. "Fall seven times, rise eight," goes the Japanese proverb — and in that single phrase lies the mastery blueprint.

Marketers, too, must fall often and rise quickly. Campaigns fail, messages miss, products flop. Yet, when studied with humility, the failure becomes a dojo of its own — a place where insight replaces ego. The advertising archives are filled with such lessons: Coca-Cola's "New Coke" debacle in 1985, or Pepsi's Kendall Jenner ad in 2017. Both were failures of sensitivity, but each reshaped internal cultures toward empathy and awareness.

Behavioral science calls this antifragility, a term popularized by Nassim Nicholas Taleb: systems that grow stronger under stress. Martial arts have embodied this principle for centuries. Each defeat, each setback, builds callus, clarity, and calm. The resilient marketer operates in the same way, using crisis not to crumble but to recalibrate.

As the martial artist learns to absorb impact, so too must the marketer learn to absorb feedback. Both understand that resilience is not the absence of pain — it is the transformation of it.

Reading Intent: Understanding Consumer and Competitor Moves

A skilled martial artist sees what is invisible to the untrained eye. Before the punch is thrown, they see the intention in the breath, the shift in weight, the widening of stance. This anticipatory perception — *zanshin* in Japanese — is cultivated through thousands of hours of attentive practice.

For marketers, *zanshin* translates to consumer insight. It's the ability to detect faint signals — a subtle change in online sentiment, a quiet surge in niche interest — before competitors even notice. Companies like Spotify, which tailor daily playlists by reading micro-behaviors in listening habits, operate in this heightened awareness zone. They don't just respond to what consumers do; they sense what consumers will do next.

In competitive markets, this level of perception can mean survival. Sun Tzu's ancient dictum from The Art of War — "Know the enemy and know yourself" — remains as relevant in brand strategy as it was in battle. But the enemy, in marketing, is not another company; it is misunderstanding. The marketer's greatest weapon, like the martial artist's, is perception sharpened by empathy.

Great marketing strategists read markets the way martial artists read opponents: not through aggression, but through attunement.

Embracing Change: From Karate Styles to Marketing Channels

Walk through the history of martial arts, and you'll find constant reinvention. When Jigoro Kano founded Judo in 1882, he stripped away Jujutsu's lethal techniques and created a modern art of learning through leverage. Bruce Lee did something similar with Jeet Kune Do — dissolving boundaries between styles, declaring that the "truth in combat" lies beyond tradition.

Marketing has undergone the same metamorphosis. From print and radio to television, then digital, and now AI-driven personalization, every era has demanded new stances. Those who clung to form — like those who refused to evolve in the dojo — became obsolete.

The emergence of "agile marketing," with its iterative sprints and cross-functional squads, mirrors the adaptability of mixed martial arts. Where older corporate structures were rigid like karate, modern teams blend tactics fluidly like MMA. The principle remains the same: survival belongs to those who evolve.

Harvard Business Review studies confirm that adaptable organizations outperform static ones by 30% in volatile markets. The martial artist's creed — be ready for any attack — has become the marketer's modern mantra: be ready for any change.

Combining Strengths: The Mixed Martial Arts of Modern Marketing

Mixed martial arts (MMA) revolutionized combat by integrating diverse traditions, including boxing, wrestling, judo, and Muay Thai, into a holistic system. The new fighter was not a specialist, but a strategist. In the same way, the modern marketer must synthesize across silos — blending analytics with storytelling, behavioral economics with creativity, and human intuition with AI.

Think of this as the MMA of Marketing. The data scientist brings precision, the creative brings emotion, the strategist brings perspective, and the brand leader integrates them into one fluid movement. This multidimensional fluency is what separates today's marketing masters from yesterday's tacticians.

Companies like Nike and Apple exemplify this synthesis. They fuse design, data, and emotion so seamlessly that their messages strike with the power of a well-timed kick — effortless, yet devastatingly effective.

The age of pure specialists has passed. The future belongs to the integrators — the mixed martial artists of meaning.

Preemptive and Reactive Strategies: "Offense" Versus "Defense" in Branding

In martial arts, some fighters dominate through offense — aggressive strikes and initiative. Others rely on defense — absorbing attacks, countering with precision. Both approaches have merit, depending on timing, opponent, and energy.

The same duality exists in marketing. A preemptive strategy — launching new products or shaping markets before anyone else — mirrors the offensive fighter. Apple's first iPhone launch in 2007 was a preemptive strike that redefined an entire category. In contrast, defensive branding — reputation management, customer retention, and trust repair — mirrors the graceful defender who neutralizes an attack without aggression.

Behavioral research from the Ehrenberg-Bass Institute supports the value of balance: brands that combine proactive innovation with strong defensive loyalty programs outperform those that focus on a single approach.

The key lies in timing. In combat, strike too early, and you overextend; react too late, and you're cornered. In branding, move too fast, and you alienate your audience; move too slow, and you fade from relevance. The strategist's art, like the fighter's, lies in sensing momentum — knowing when to attack and when to yield.

The Strategic Parallel

Strategy in both martial arts and marketing is less about domination and more about harmonization. It's about understanding rhythm — the tempo of a fight, the cadence of a market — and aligning your movements to it.

Bruce Lee once said, "It's not the daily increase but the daily decrease — hack away at the unessential." That is perhaps the deepest strategic wisdom both arts share. The master, whether on the mat or in the marketplace, succeeds not by doing more, but by doing precisely what matters most.

Section 6

Values at the Core

Discipline in Execution and Follow-Through

In the dojo, discipline is not an abstract virtue — it is the rhythm of progress. Every bow, every stance, every repetition reinforces the same idea: mastery is not a moment, but a method. A martial artist doesn't wait for motivation; they act out of ritual.

Marketing, too, rewards discipline far more than inspiration. The most successful campaigns are not always the most creative — they are the most consistent. Consider the global success of Nike's *Just Do It* or Dove's *Real Beauty*. These ideas have endured for decades not because they were loud, but because they were lived — executed with disciplined precision across every medium, every message, every era.

Execution discipline in marketing mirrors the martial artist's focus during form practice. It is easy to get distracted by trends, analytics dashboards, or flashy ideas. But true mastery, as any sensei would say, lies in refining fundamentals. The marketer's kata — the daily rhythm of planning, implementing, measuring, and refining — builds a form of quiet excellence.

Behavioral science supports this connection. Psychologist Angela Duckworth's research on grit shows that sustained effort, not brilliance, predicts long-term success. Both the black belt and the market leader earn their rank the same way: through follow-through, persistence, and an unwavering respect for the process.

Respect — For Teachers, Peers, Customers, and Competitors

Every martial art begins and ends with a bow. It is a small act, but within it lies a profound truth: respect precedes technique. The bow is not submission — it is acknowledgment. It honors lineage, learning, and the shared pursuit of excellence.

Marketing, when practiced ethically, is an act of respect as well. It honors the customer's intelligence, the competitor's craft, and the market's complexity. Great marketers — like great martial artists — understand that their art exists in relationship, not isolation.

Companies that practice respect as a strategy tend to endure. Toyota's customer-centric philosophy, grounded in the Japanese principle of *genchi genbutsu* ("go and see for yourself"), mirrors the martial artist's respect for firsthand experience. This is why Toyota remains a benchmark for trust and reliability worldwide.

Respect also extends to competitors. Bruce Lee once said that an opponent is not an enemy but a mirror — reflecting your own strengths and weaknesses. The same holds in the marketplace. Pepsi's existence sharpened Coca-Cola's storytelling; Apple's rivalry with Microsoft fueled creativity and courage. True respect is competitive admiration — iron sharpening iron.

Humility and Ego Management

Perhaps the most misunderstood aspect of martial arts is that it is not about dominance, but control — not of others, but of oneself. The master, contrary to stereotype, is rarely boastful. Their power is quiet, their confidence understated.

Marketers, however, operate in a culture that often rewards visibility over virtue. The temptation of ego — the drive to claim originality, to "own" the narrative — can blind even the most brilliant strategist. Yet history shows that humility, not hubris, builds longevity.

Consider Old Spice. Once an aging brand, it reinvented itself in 2010 with humor and self-awareness, embracing irony rather than clinging to pride. The result: a viral success that redefined an entire category. That campaign worked not because the brand boasted, but because it listened.

In both disciplines, humility keeps learning alive. As Zen masters often remind their students: "The cup must be empty to be filled." The marketer who assumes they know their audience has already stopped learning. The martial artist who assumes they've mastered their art has already begun to decline.

Neuroscientists refer to this as the beginner's mind — an openness that enhances neuroplasticity, thereby keeping the brain adaptive. The humble practitioner, whether on the mat or in the market, evolves faster because they remain teachable.

Courage and Taking Calculated Risks

No martial artist can progress without courage. The first sparring session is an act of faith — stepping into the unknown, facing controlled chaos, trusting instinct. Courage is not the absence of fear, but the ability to act in its presence.

Marketing, too, demands courage — to launch a radical idea, challenge convention, or reveal vulnerability in an industry that prizes certainty. Dove's "Real Beauty" campaign challenged entrenched beauty norms. Apple's "Think Different" dared audiences to reject conformity. In each case, courage wasn't reckless; it was calculated.

Psychological studies on risk-taking show that the most effective leaders are not gamblers but measured experimenters. They take small, disciplined risks to test hypotheses, then scale what works. This is the martial artist's philosophy of controlled exposure: incrementally increasing challenge to build both skill and confidence.

The martial artist learns to breathe through fear. The marketer learns to breathe through uncertainty. Both discover that courage, when anchored in preparation, becomes not a gamble but a strategy.

Mastery as a Journey, Not a Destination

In both arts, the highest achievement is not arrival but awareness. The black belt is not the end of training but the beginning of teaching. The world's best marketers know this feeling well — success opens new questions rather than closing them.

Mastery, as defined by the martial philosopher Gichin Funakoshi, is "to seek perfection of character." In marketing, mastery means seeking perfection of purpose — ensuring every action aligns with the brand's essence, and the audience's good.

Harvard psychologist Ellen Langer's research on mindfulness echoes this view: true expertise is not rigid repetition but active engagement — a continuous recalibration to the present moment. The martial artist and marketer alike must remain awake, curious, and responsive to change.

Ultimately, mastery is a mirror. It reflects who we are becoming, not what we have achieved. The martial artist refines movement to reveal mind; the marketer refines message to reveal meaning. Both, at their best, practice not the art of winning, but the art of becoming.

The Ethical Heart of Both Arts

At the deepest level, martial arts and marketing share the same moral architecture: discipline in action, respect in competition, humility in learning, courage in execution, and the pursuit of mastery as a lifelong path.

The greatest martial masters taught that the ultimate victory is harmony — not conquest. The greatest marketers, consciously or not, seek the same: to harmonize brands and humanity, commerce and conscience, persuasion and purpose.

Both understand that strength without ethics is fragility disguised as power — and that the true measure of mastery is how one uses it.

Section 7

Real-World Examples & Case Studies

UFC and Social Media: Fighters as Masterful Personal Brands

The Ultimate Fighting Championship (UFC) is often seen as raw, primal combat — a spectacle of strength and will. But beneath the blood and bravado lies one of the most sophisticated branding laboratories of the 21st century. Every fighter, knowingly or not, is a marketer.

Conor McGregor is the most visible example. His mastery of personal branding transformed him from a local Dublin boxer into a global phenomenon. Like Muhammad Ali before him, McGregor understood that narrative—not just a knockout — wins over audiences. His flamboyance, his rhythm of speech, his rivalry-fueled storytelling — all mirror the same psychological principles that marketers use to build anticipation, emotional resonance, and loyalty.

UFC's model thrives on storytelling archetypes: the underdog, the technician, the showman, the comeback hero. Each fight is a miniature campaign, built around narrative tension and resolution. Social media amplifies this structure; fighters cultivate parasocial relationships with fans, offering behind-the-scenes authenticity that humanizes the spectacle.

For marketers, the UFC offers a masterclass in identity-based branding. It demonstrates how consistency of character, emotional authenticity, and audience engagement can turn individuals — or companies — into movements.

As in martial arts, strength in marketing today lies not merely in power, but in presence.

The Garage Beer "Brewmit" Campaign: Martial Arts Storytelling in Marketing

In 2018, Garage Beer, a small craft brewery in Spain, launched a campaign that would become a cult favorite in advertising circles. Their challenge: compete with multinational giants with budgets hundreds of times larger. Their solution: become the underdog warrior.

They created "Brewmite," a fictional martial artist monk who had devoted his life to perfecting one beer — not ten, not fifty, but one. The campaign was filmed in cinematic style, parodying 1970s kung fu movies, complete with training montages, ancient wisdom, and the line: "True mastery needs only one strike."

The humor was self-aware, but the message was profound: focus, discipline, and mastery over excess. Sales surged 40% within three months, and brand recall tripled.

Psychologists would describe this as narrative transportation — when audiences emotionally enter a story, they suspend disbelief and internalize its message. Brewmite embodied the martial ethos: that restraint and refinement trump abundance.

What Garage Beer understood — and what many marketers forget — is that stories of mastery, humility, and purpose cut through the noise. In a world addicted to more, the brand that preaches less — but better — wins hearts.

Bruce Lee's "Be Like Water": Adaptability as a Marketing Philosophy

Few quotes have traveled as far, across so many domains, as Bruce Lee's "Be like water." Originally spoken as a metaphor for martial adaptability, it has since become a touchstone for design thinking, innovation, and even leadership philosophy.

In marketing, the "Be like water" ethos is embodied by brands that refuse rigidity. Netflix pivoted from DVD rentals to streaming, then from content distribution to original creation — a transformation driven by fluid adaptation to audience behavior. Similarly, Spotify evolved from a simple music library into an ecosystem of personalization, curating moments rather than merely songs.

Lee's insight was not just poetic — it was predictive. Behavioral economists have shown that adaptability is the single most reliable indicator of long-term success in volatile markets. Flexibility allows brands to navigate obstacles — technological shifts, social change, or global crises — rather than resist them.

To "be like water" in marketing is to remain humble in the face of cultural currents. It's to listen, move, and evolve — not to dominate the environment, but to move with it.

BJJ (Brazilian Jiu-Jitsu) Schools: Grassroots Marketing and Community Building

Brazilian Jiu-Jitsu (BJJ) began as a localized martial art in Rio de Janeiro's favelas, developed by the Gracie family. It grew globally not through mass advertising, but through demonstration, storytelling, and community.

Each BJJ school functions as a tribe — small, intimate, fiercely loyal. Members share transformation stories: weight loss, regained confidence, and learned resilience. These personal testimonials became the art's most powerful marketing engine.

In marketing terms, BJJ is a case study in community-based growth. Word-of-mouth, not mass media, built its empire. Every practitioner is both student and ambassador — the perfect embodiment of earned media.

Modern brands like CrossFit and Peloton replicate this model. They create micro-communities around shared struggle and personal evolution — both echoing the martial arts philosophy that mastery is communal, not competitive.

The BJJ model reminds marketers that authenticity is scalable — not through volume, but through depth. Connection always beats conversion.

Martial Arts Events: Leveraging Tournaments and Demos for Local Brand Growth

Small martial arts schools have long mastered local experiential marketing — long before the term existed. Tournaments, belt ceremonies, and community demonstrations are not just events; they are brand touchpoints. Each one reinforces credibility, culture, and continuity.

Similarly, local brands thrive when they transform marketing from broadcast to embodied experience. A farmer's market, a fitness pop-up, or a microbrew tasting event functions like a martial arts exhibition — a live performance of values.

Neuroscientists studying the embodied cognition theory argue that experiences encoded through action and participation are remembered longer than passive information. This is why experiential marketing consistently outperforms traditional advertising in recall and emotional resonance.

The martial arts community intuitively knew this. Every demo is a story performed, every belt test a ritual of proof. In both arts, participation transforms audiences into believers.

Cross-Promotions: Fitness, Self-Defense, and Lifestyle Branding Collaboration

Over the last decade, martial arts brands have successfully integrated with broader lifestyle trends, including wellness, mindfulness, and empowerment. From Adidas's "Combat Sports" apparel line to Lululemon's partnerships with mixed martial arts influencers, the integration reflects a cultural shift: martial arts is no longer about fighting; it's about becoming.

Marketers have learned to reposition martial imagery from aggression to growth. Campaigns that once glorified combat now celebrate confidence, control, and calm. This reframing mirrors what modern consumers crave: not dominance, but balance.

Collaborations between martial arts schools and wellness brands — yoga studios, meditation apps, nutrition lines — demonstrate a cross-disciplinary synergy. Each borrows credibility from the other, creating a hybrid narrative of physical, emotional, and ethical strength.

For marketers, this convergence is instructive: when you align your brand's story with a higher purpose, you stop selling and start transforming.

Historical Brand Positioning Battles Mirroring Martial Arts Rivalries

History's great marketing rivalries — such as Coca-Cola vs. Pepsi, Apple vs. Microsoft, and Nike vs. Adidas — mirror the legendary rivalries of martial arts schools. Each begins with philosophy, evolves through competition, and ends in mutual respect.

Coke's narrative of timeless authenticity faced Pepsi's youthful rebellion. Apple's simplicity challenged Microsoft's functionality. Nike's emotional storytelling countered Adidas's athletic credibility. Each duel forced evolution — a perpetual sparring match of innovation.

In martial arts, rivalries like Shotokan vs. Goju-Ryu or Kung Fu vs. Karate did the same. Philosophical contrasts fueled innovation, pushing each school to define and refine its essence.

The lesson for marketers is timeless: rivalry refines identity. Without competition, purpose blurs. The best brands — like the best fighters — use opposition not for destruction but for definition.

The Living Proof of the Parallel

Across all these cases runs a single current: martial arts principles do not merely metaphorically apply to marketing — they functionally do. The same dynamics of discipline, adaptability, resilience, and authenticity that define martial excellence also define enduring brands.

Every dojo teaches that the fight is not against others but against complacency. Every great marketing campaign teaches the same: mastery lies in never ceasing to learn, listen, and evolve.

Section 8

Application Toolkit

Applying the Martial Arts Mindset to Campaign Planning

In martial arts, the first thing a student learns is stance — not how to punch or kick, but how to stand. Without balance, every motion collapses. The same is true in marketing. Before tactics or tools come into play, a campaign must have balance — a steady stance built on insight, strategy, and intent.

This is where marketers can borrow the dojo discipline of planning. Every campaign begins not with brainstorming, but with centering. What is the purpose? What values must guide it? Who is the "opponent"—the problem, the market inertia, the consumer doubt—we must overcome?

Just as a martial artist visualizes each move before the match, marketers who visualize the consumer journey before execution perform better. A 2021 Harvard Business Review study found that teams that spent 20% more time on planning achieved 30% higher creative effectiveness and ROI. Preparation, it turns out, is a competitive advantage — on the mat and in the marketplace alike.

Campaign planning, then, is not an act of imagination alone. It is a ritual of alignment. Like bowing before sparring, it signals respect — for the craft, the customer, and the challenge ahead.

Developing a "Marketing Kata": Rituals for Consistency

In traditional dojos, kata — sequences of practiced movements — are more than drills. They are codified wisdom, designed to train instinct through repetition. Each motion embodies centuries of refinement. The practitioner learns not just what to do, but how to think.

Marketers can build their own kata — a series of rituals that cultivate consistency, clarity, and reflection. For example:

- Morning kata: reviewing campaign dashboards, insights, and competitive movements.
- Weekly kata: assessing creative alignment with core brand values.

- Monthly kata: running retrospectives to identify what worked, what didn't, and why.
- Quarterly kata: re-centering strategy around changing audience needs.

These are not bureaucratic checklists — they are forms of mindfulness. They keep teams grounded in rhythm and responsibility, ensuring that creativity does not drift into chaos.

Toyota's Kaizen philosophy — continuous incremental improvement — was directly inspired by martial discipline. Its success in both manufacturing and marketing is proof that excellence grows not from bursts of innovation, but from ritualized attention to detail.

The martial artist perfects form through repetition; the marketer perfects relevance through routine.

Training Drills: From Pitch Practice to Campaign War-Gaming

In the dojo, sparring prepares one for the unpredictability of real combat. No amount of theory replaces the jolt of real-time reaction — the moment an opponent breaks your rhythm, and you must adapt instinctively.

Marketing teams can simulate this same dynamic through campaign drills and war-gaming. Before a product launch, for instance, teams can run mock press releases, crisis scenarios, or counter-campaigns against competitors. The goal isn't fear, but fluency — to develop instinctive agility under pressure.

Unilever and Procter & Gamble famously use "brand war rooms" — immersive sessions where marketers, strategists, and creatives anticipate every potential challenge. These are marketing's sparring sessions: a space to test resilience, timing, and adaptability.

Cognitive psychologists call this mental simulation — rehearsing possible futures to strengthen decision-making networks in the brain. Military strategists have long used it; martial artists live by it; marketers can thrive through it.

The key is to transform reaction into readiness — so that when disruption strikes, it feels like déjà vu, not disaster.

Measuring Progress: Setting Belts and Milestones in Marketing Teams

In martial arts, belts symbolize not just skill but consistency. The white belt isn't about ignorance — it represents openness, the beginning of learning. The black belt isn't mastery — it's mastery of fundamentals, and the humility to start over.

Imagine if marketing teams measured growth this way — not through vanity metrics like impressions or reach, but through developmental milestones. A "white belt" marketer might learn campaign mechanics; a "blue belt" might master audience segmentation; a "brown belt" might lead cross-channel storytelling; a "black belt" might integrate strategy, psychology, and technology into seamless brand orchestration.

Google's "Digital Garage" training programs, HubSpot's certification tiers, and Adobe's professional learning paths all echo this belt philosophy — turning learning into a journey, not a checklist.

Even internally, some companies are adopting symbolic "belt levels" to recognize mastery in analytics, leadership, or storytelling. It creates a culture where improvement is celebrated, not imposed.

Progress, in both arts, is not about speed — it's about direction. The belt reminds us that what matters is not how quickly we climb, but how deeply we grow.

From Practice to Philosophy

Each of these tools — the campaign kata, the sparring drill, the belt system — is more than a metaphor. It is a method for transforming marketing from a mere activity into an art form. It's easy to think of campaigns as battles and consumers as opponents, but the martial lens offers a deeper view: marketing is a discipline of awareness.

When teams internalize the martial mindset, their work shifts from reactionary to intentional, from fragmented to focused. They stop chasing the latest tools and start mastering timeless principles — awareness, precision, timing, and respect.

In the end, what separates a master marketer from a novice is not the number of campaigns launched, but the quality of attention brought to each one. As the great martial philosopher Miyamoto Musashi wrote in The Book of Five Rings:

"The way is in training."

So it is in marketing. Every campaign is practice. Every mistake is a lesson. Every success is a momentary stance in the long kata of mastery.

Section 9

Pitfalls and Misconceptions

Over-Specialization: Narrow Marketing Channels vs. Mixed Approaches

Every martial artist begins by mastering one form — karate, judo, taekwondo. But the masters who endure learn to transcend form altogether. Bruce Lee called it the art of fighting without fighting — a rejection of rigidity. He argued that clinging to a single style creates predictability, and predictability breeds defeat.

Marketers fall into the same trap. In a landscape overflowing with data dashboards, social platforms, and marketing technology (martech) tools, specialization feels safe. The SEO expert, the influencer strategist, the performance marketer — each wields great skill within a narrow domain. Yet, when the environment shifts, over-specialization becomes a liability.

The pandemic revealed this brutally. Brands that relied solely on event marketing or retail presence collapsed when the world moved online. Those that had diversified—mastering digital storytelling, omnichannel engagement, and community building —adapted seamlessly.

The martial artist who trains only in offense will falter when forced to defend. The marketer who invests only in one channel will flounder when the algorithm changes. Balance, not bias, is the key.

A McKinsey study in 2022 found that "adaptive generalists" — teams skilled across creative, analytical, and strategic dimensions — outperform pure specialists by 33% in volatile markets. The lesson echoes martial wisdom: technique matters less than timing, and timing comes from understanding all forms.

The future belongs to what Bruce Lee called the formless form—marketers who are not confined by platforms but guided by purpose.

"Winning" in Marketing — What does Success Really Mean?

In martial arts, the notion of "winning" is more complex than victory. The opponent is a mirror, not an enemy. Every sparring match teaches humility, rhythm, and restraint. The true victory is mastery over impulse — the ability to remain calm amid chaos.

Marketing, too, often confuses winning with visibility. A viral campaign, a trending hashtag, a burst of engagement — these are the equivalent of the knockout punch: impressive, fleeting, and often superficial. Real success, like mastery, is measured differently — in trust, in longevity, in the quiet power of consistency.

Consider Patagonia. It has never chased virality; its messaging is slow, deliberate, and moral. Yet its influence is immense. Or take Apple — rarely reactive, seldom loud, always focused on design and experience. Both brands understand what many marketers forget: you can win attention and still lose meaning.

Martial arts philosophy warns against obsession with the scoreboard. In Judo, there's a term — *shiai* — meaning "meeting of wills." Victory here is relational, not absolute. Marketing operates the same way. The brand's goal is not to defeat the consumer's defenses, but to engage their trust.

"Winning," in its deepest sense, is harmony — between product and promise, brand and belief, purpose and performance.

Confusing Activity with Impact

In a world that rewards constant motion, stillness feels like failure. Marketers fill calendars with content, social posts, and product updates — often mistaking busyness for progress. But as any martial artist knows, flurries of movement without intent are wasted energy.

The untrained fighter attacks relentlessly, exhausting themselves before the match is halfway done. The master waits — poised, patient, precise. One well-timed strike achieves what a hundred chaotic punches cannot.

Marketing suffers from a similar illusion. Flooding the market with messages, emails, and ads may create noise, but not necessarily resonance. True impact requires rhythm — the right message, at the right time, in the right place.

Neuroscience provides evidence for this. Studies on attention fatigue show that oversaturation dulls emotional response. Consumers, overwhelmed by stimuli, disengage. In contrast, strategic minimalism — carefully timed, emotionally charged communication — heightens attention and recall.

Think of Apple's *Think Different*, Nike's *Just Do It*, or Dove's *Real Beauty*. These weren't frequent campaigns; they were focused ones. Each landed like a perfect strike — memorable because it was measured.

The martial arts lesson here is timeless: movement without mindfulness weakens both art and artist. The same holds for marketing. Less movement, more meaning. Less noise, more nuance.

The Ego Trap: Mistaking Control for Mastery

One of the subtlest pitfalls in both martial arts and marketing is ego — the illusion of control. The martial artist who believes they've mastered the art stops learning. The marketer who believes they've mastered the market stops listening.

Ego seduces through success. A viral hit, a record quarter, an award — each one reinforces the myth of mastery. But in truth, the market, like the opponent, is never static. Conditions change. Consumer values shift. What once worked becomes irrelevant.

The martial arts creed teaches surrender: You do not control the fight; you harmonize with it. The best marketers live by the same principle. They don't dominate markets; they flow with them — sensing undercurrents of change and adjusting accordingly.

The more power a brand gains, the greater its responsibility to remain humble. As the Zen proverb says, "When the student is ready, the teacher appears. When the master is ready, the student reappears." In other words: mastery is a circle, not a summit.

The Ultimate Misconception: Mistaking Mastery for Arrival

Both marketers and martial artists risk believing that mastery is an endpoint — a belt, a title, a viral campaign. But mastery, as every true practitioner learns, is not arrival — it's awareness. It's the capacity to stay attuned in a changing world.

In 1964, after defeating multiple opponents in Hong Kong, Bruce Lee wrote in his diary:

"The highest technique is to have no technique. My style is no style."

It was both a confession and a philosophy. The same could be said of great marketing today. The highest technique is not a tactic but a truth: to know the consumer so well that persuasion becomes empathy.

Every campaign, like every sparring match, is temporary. The real work begins after — in reflection, refinement, and readiness for what comes next.

In the end, the marketer's greatest pitfall is forgetting that the art itself is alive. It breathes, evolves, and mirrors the times. To stay relevant is not to fight harder, but to listen deeper.

Section 10

Conclusion

The Path to Mastery: Lifelong Learning in Both Fields

At the heart of both martial arts and marketing lies the same paradox: the more one learns, the more one realizes how much remains unseen. The martial artist, decades into training, still returns to the same forms — only now, they notice subtleties invisible to their younger self. The marketer, years into building brands, finds that every new campaign teaches old lessons anew: that timing matters more than technology, that empathy outlasts algorithms, that attention must be earned, not bought.

Mastery, in both realms, is not an ascent to the top but a spiral — revisiting fundamentals with deeper awareness each time around. As Bruce Lee said, "I fear not the man who has practiced 10,000 kicks once, but the man who has practiced one kick 10,000 times." The modern marketer could say the same: the power is not in the number of campaigns launched, but in how consciously each one is crafted, measured, and evolved.

Research on deliberate practice confirms what these traditions have long known. Psychologist Anders Ericsson demonstrated that world-class expertise emerges only after thousands of hours of purposeful, feedback-rich, reflective, and self-aware repetition. The dojo and the marketing lab share this same rhythm: learn, test, refine, repeat. It's not glamorous, but it's transformative.

Mastery, then, is less about what one knows and more about how one learns. It's an ongoing relationship with curiosity — a commitment to refinement that never ends.

Evolving Together: What the Future Holds for Martial-Artists-Turned-Marketers

In an era where artificial intelligence can write ads, predict behavior, and even simulate empathy, it might seem that the human marketer — like the traditional martial artist — risks obsolescence. But that assumption misunderstands both arts. The point of mastery has never been to outdo others, but to understand oneself.

Technology, like a powerful weapon, magnifies both wisdom and recklessness. Without discipline, it breeds noise; with discipline, it becomes an extension of human insight. The martial artist learns to use the sword only after mastering restraint; the marketer must master purpose before mastering automation.

The future will reward philosophical marketers — those who balance data with discernment, algorithms with empathy, and speed with stillness. In this sense, tomorrow's best marketers will resemble martial artists more than engineers: calm amid chaos, fluent in adaptation, and guided by principles, not just processes.

We can already see this evolution unfolding. The brands that endure — Patagonia, Apple, Nike, LEGO — operate with a martial sense of identity. They know who they are, what they stand for, and when to move. Their campaigns are not reactive outbursts but disciplined strikes, aligned with long-term purpose.

Just as martial arts integrate mind, body, and spirit, the marketer of the future must integrate creativity, analytics, and ethics. Without this harmony, campaigns may win clicks — but lose meaning.

Harmony Over Victory

In the final analysis, both martial arts and marketing teach that true strength lies not in domination, but in harmony. The greatest masters seek not to destroy opponents but to neutralize conflict — to restore balance.

Marketing, too, is at its noblest when it harmonizes commerce and conscience, profit and purpose. When Dove tells women they are beautiful as they are, or when REI closes its stores on Black Friday to encourage time outdoors, these are not just campaigns — they are gestures of balance, of aligning brand with belief.

The dojo and the boardroom share this moral terrain. Both are places where power must meet humility, where precision must meet empathy. Both ask the same question: What do we serve — the self, or the whole?

Mastery and Market Dominance: The Same Discipline, Different Arena

The martial artist and the marketer walk parallel paths. One disciplines the body to act without hesitation; the other disciplines the mind to decide without confusion. Both depend on clarity — of purpose, of perception, of principle.

Market dominance, in its truest sense, is not about control or conquest. It's about resonance. The brand that achieves mastery doesn't shout the loudest — it speaks the truest. It becomes part of cultural rhythm, embedded in memory the way a kata lives in muscle.

Think of Nike's eternal three words: Just Do It. Or Apple's two-word rebellion: Think Different. These are not slogans. They are mantras, repeated like martial incantations until they transcend category and enter culture.

Dominance, then, is not an outcome. It's an alignment between vision, value, and voice. The brand, like the martial artist, moves from technique to intuition, from performance to presence.

The Circle Closes: Marketing as Modern Martial Art

In the end, the dojo and the marketplace are reflections of the same human striving — the pursuit of mastery through awareness, discipline, and purpose. Both ask the practitioner to study motion, energy, and timing; to act without waste; to compete without hatred; to seek perfection not in others, but in oneself.

The masters of either domain know that the real opponent is not outside — it's inertia, ego, and distraction. The path forward is inward.

When marketers learn to approach their craft the way martial artists approach their practice — with reverence, patience, and precision — marketing ceases to be manipulation and becomes meditation.

The ancient samurai saying captures it best:

"In the midst of chaos, there is also opportunity. But only for the calm mind."

That is the marketer's final lesson from the martial arts: calm is not the absence of motion — it is mastery within it. And mastery, in every age and every discipline, is the most enduring form of power there is.

Ten Key Lessons Marketers can Learn from Martial Arts

Lesson 1: Mastery Begins with Mastering the Basics

In every dojo, the beginner is surprised by something.

Not by flying kicks.

Not by complex joint locks.

Not by advanced sparring drills.

But by repetition.

The white belt spends weeks learning how to stand.

How to breathe.

How to bow.

How to step forward without losing balance.

At first, it feels too simple.

But mastery begins there.

The Illusion of Advanced Technique

In marketing, we are often seduced by sophistication:

- AI-driven personalization
- Omnichannel orchestration
- Viral campaigns
- Influencer ecosystems
- Growth hacking frameworks

These tools have value.

But they do not replace fundamentals.

A martial artist who neglects stance cannot execute a powerful strike.

A marketer who neglects fundamentals cannot build enduring brands.

Before automation, there must be clarity.

Before amplification, there must be positioning.

Before scale, there must be trust.

The Marketing Basics Most Often Ignored

Mastery in marketing rests on a few foundational disciplines:

- **Clear Value Proposition**: Can you articulate, in one sentence, why your brand matters?
- **Deep Customer Understanding**: Do you understand your customer's pain, aspiration, and context — not just demographics?
- **Consistent Messaging:** Does every touchpoint reinforce the same core idea?
- **Strong Execution**: Are campaigns implemented with discipline and follow-through?
- **Measurement and Reflection**: Do you learn from outcomes and refine accordingly?

These are not glamorous.

But they are powerful.

Repetition Builds Instinct

In martial arts, repetition builds muscle memory.

In marketing, repetition builds market memory.

Consistency of message — over years — creates recognition. Recognition creates trust. Trust creates preference.

Brands that chase novelty without mastering fundamentals often exhaust themselves.

They experiment endlessly, but fail to anchor identity.

The black belt returns to basic drills daily.

The master marketer revisits fundamentals regularly.

The Discipline of Refinement

Mastery is not about performing basics once.

It is about refining them continuously.

A stance can always improve.

A message can always be sharpened.

A customer insight can deepen.

Toyota's Kaizen philosophy reminds us: small improvements compound.

Nike's repetition of "Just Do It" reminds us: disciplined consistency builds equity.

Apple's minimalist messaging reminds us: clarity is power.

All great brands, at their core, have mastered simplicity.

The Ego Trap

The greatest obstacle to mastering basics is ego.

We want to feel advanced.

We want to implement complex strategies.

We want to innovate visibly.

But skipping fundamentals creates fragility.

In the dojo, overconfidence invites imbalance.

In marketing, premature complexity invites confusion.

True mastery requires humility — the willingness to return to foundational drills.

The Compounding Effect

Small refinements, practiced consistently, compound over time.

- Slightly clearer messaging
- Slightly sharper targeting
- Slightly stronger creative discipline
- Slightly better post-campaign analysis

These incremental gains create exponential outcomes.

The black belt was once a white belt who did not give up on the basics.

Closing Reflection

Mastery does not begin with scale.

It begins with stance.

Before you seek innovation, seek clarity.

Before you chase virality, strengthen fundamentals.

Before you attempt advanced techniques, perfect the first movement.

In martial arts and in marketing,

the path to dominance

starts on the ground.

And those who bow to the basics rise to mastery.

Lesson 2: Discipline Outperforms Talent

In every dojo, there are two kinds of students.

The naturally gifted.

And the relentlessly disciplined.

At first, the gifted student dazzles.

Faster reflexes.

Sharper coordination.

Quicker grasp of technique.

But as months turn into years, something predictable happens.

The disciplined student overtakes the talented one.

Because talent flashes.

Discipline endures.

The Myth of Natural Ability

In martial arts, talent can provide an early advantage.

Flexibility. Strength. Speed.

But without disciplined practice, talent plateaus.

The same is true in marketing.

Some professionals possess instinctive creativity. Others have intuitive strategic thinking. Some can craft headlines effortlessly.

But creativity without structure leads to inconsistency.

Insight without execution leads to unrealized potential.

Markets reward consistency more than flashes of brilliance.

Discipline as Structured Repetition

Discipline is not dramatic.

It is repetitive.

- Weekly reviews of campaign performance
- Consistent adherence to brand guidelines
- Regular customer research updates
- Post-mortem analyses after launches

These practices lack glamour.

But they build cumulative strength.

In martial arts, repetition sharpens technique until movement becomes instinct.

In marketing, disciplined processes sharpen strategy until decision-making becomes precise.

Talent Seeks Applause. Discipline Seeks Improvement.

The talented marketer may chase breakthrough ideas.

The disciplined marketer refines fundamentals.

The talented team celebrates creativity.

The disciplined team measures outcomes.

Over time, discipline compounds. Talent alone does not.

- Nike's consistency over decades demonstrates disciplined message reinforcement.
- Toyota's Kaizen culture demonstrates disciplined operational refinement.
- Oreo's real-time agility was made possible by disciplined preparation.

None of these successes were accidents of talent.

They were outcomes of structure.

The Quiet Power of Routine

In the dojo, daily drills matter more than tournament victories.

In marketing, operational rigor matters more than occasional viral success.

Discipline appears in small habits:

- Documenting insights
- Maintaining message coherence

- Protecting brand tone
- Following through on commitments

These habits build credibility internally and externally.

When teams rely solely on talent, results fluctuate.

When teams rely on discipline, performance stabilizes and strengthens.

Discipline Under Pressure

Talent often falters in adversity.

Discipline steadies.

When campaigns underperform, disciplined teams analyze calmly.

When markets shift, disciplined leaders reassess systematically.

When competition intensifies, disciplined brands remain anchored in purpose.

In martial arts, composure under pressure defines mastery.

In marketing, disciplined resilience defines longevity.

The Ego Barrier

Talent feeds ego.

Discipline tempers it.

The gifted practitioner may resist correction.

The disciplined practitioner seeks it.

Marketing teams driven by ego defend ideas.

Disciplined teams refine them.

Mastery requires the humility to repeat drills long after applause fades.

Compounding Consistency

Discipline produces incremental gains that accumulate:

- Slightly stronger brand recall
- Slightly improved customer retention
- Slightly clearer positioning

Over the years, these small advantages widen the competitive distance.

Talent may win a campaign.

Discipline builds a legacy.

Closing Reflection

In martial arts, black belts are not awarded for talent.

They are awarded for perseverance.

Marketing mastery follows the same law.

Talent may open doors.

Discipline keeps them open.

The practitioner who shows up daily, refines basics relentlessly, and measures progress honestly will surpass the naturally gifted who rely on instinct alone.

In the arena of markets, discipline is not restraint.

It is power.

And power practiced consistently becomes mastery.

Lesson 3: Adaptability is Strength — "Be Like Water"

In martial arts, rigidity is a liability.

The stiff fighter resists change.

The fluid fighter adjusts.

When pressure comes, water does not resist the rock.

It flows around it.

This philosophy — famously articulated by Bruce Lee — captures one of the deepest truths of both combat and commerce:

Strength is not hardness.

Strength is adaptability.

The Illusion of Control

Many practitioners believe strength lies in force.

Many marketers believe strength lies in dominance — market share, brand visibility, and budget size.

But markets are living systems.

Consumer behavior shifts.

Technology evolves.

Cultural contexts change.

What worked yesterday may weaken tomorrow.

Rigid brands cling to past success.

Fluid brands evolve.

In the dojo, a technique that works against one opponent may fail against another.

Mastery lies not in memorizing moves, but in reading the moment.

Netflix and the Pivot Principle

Consider Netflix.

It began with DVDs.

It shifted to streaming.

It became a content creator.

Each pivot required relinquishing comfort.

Adaptability is not reactive panic.

It is an anticipatory adjustment.

Netflix did not wait for extinction.

It moved before necessity forced it.

That is martial awareness.

Adaptability Anchored in Identity

Fluidity does not mean losing center.

Water changes shape, but it remains water.

Strong brands adapt tactics while preserving philosophy.

Apple evolves devices but maintains minimalist clarity.

Nike shifts campaigns but preserves empowerment.

Spotify refreshes aesthetics but maintains personalization.

Adaptability without identity creates confusion.

Identity without adaptability creates stagnation.

Mastery requires both.

Reading the Terrain

In martial arts, terrain matters:

- Open space invites long-range strikes.
- Confined space favors grappling.
- Uneven ground demands balance adjustments.

In marketing, terrain includes:

- Cultural mood
- Economic cycles
- Platform algorithms
- Competitive behavior

Adaptable marketers observe before acting.

They ask:

What has shifted?

What remains constant?

What must be refined?

Strength lies in interpretation.

The Discipline behind Fluidity

Fluidity is often mistaken for improvisation.

In truth, it is structured flexibility.

The adaptable practitioner trains extensively.

The adaptable brand invests in data, feedback loops, and scenario planning.

Oreo's "Dunk in the Dark" worked because preparation met opportunity.

Without discipline, adaptability becomes chaos.

With discipline, it becomes an advantage.

The Fear of Change

Why do brands resist adaptation?

Fear of dilution.

Fear of failure.

Fear of losing control.

But in the dojo, fear tightens muscles, and tightening reduces responsiveness.

Relaxed awareness increases agility.

Markets reward brands that evolve confidently.

Kodak resisted digital transformation.

Toyota adapted incrementally.

Patagonia adjusts strategy while preserving purpose.

The lesson is clear: adaptation is survival refined by foresight.

Strength through Yielding

One of the paradoxes of martial arts is that yielding can neutralize force.

Judo teaches redirection rather than resistance.

In marketing, resistance to change often amplifies disruption.

Adaptable brands absorb shocks and redirect energy.

During a crisis, they recalibrate messaging.

During technological shifts, they experiment early.

Yielding strategically strengthens position.

Compounding Adaptability

Each adaptive move builds resilience:

- Updating channel strategies
- Refining messaging tone
- Responding to cultural shifts
- Adjusting pricing models

Over time, adaptability becomes a cultural habit.

Cultural habit becomes a competitive edge.

Closing Reflection

Water does not argue with the container.

It shapes itself to it.

In martial arts and in marketing, the rigid practitioner breaks under pressure.

The adaptable practitioner flows.

To “be like water” is not to be formless.

It is to be responsive without losing essence.

It is to remain centered while adjusting shape.

In dynamic markets, adaptability is not a weakness.

It is strength in motion.

And strength in motion wins the long fight.

Lesson 4: Awareness is the First Lesson you Train

Before technique, there is awareness.

Before strength, there is perception.

In every serious dojo, the first lessons are not about striking or throwing.

They are about attention.

- How you stand.
- Where your weight rests.
- How you breathe.
- What you notice.

The novice wants to move.

The master first learns to observe.

In marketing, awareness is no different.

The Discipline of Seeing Clearly

Most marketing failures do not stem from a lack of effort.

They stem from a lack of awareness.

- Launching products without understanding customer pain.
- Escalating campaigns without reading the market mood.

Copying competitors without noticing contextual differences.

Awareness means pausing long enough to ask:

What is actually happening?

In martial arts, reacting without awareness leads to imbalance.

In marketing, acting without awareness leads to waste.

Three Levels of Awareness in Marketing

Just as a martial practitioner trains to read the body, the opponent, and the environment, marketers must cultivate layered awareness.

1. **Self-Awareness**

   What are your strengths? Weaknesses? Biases?

   Is your strategy driven by data — or ego?

2. **Customer Awareness**

   What is the customer truly experiencing?

   Not what surveys say — what behaviors reveal.

3. **Market Awareness**

   What shifts are occurring in technology, regulation, culture, and competition?

   Mastery begins when observation precedes reaction.

The Ego Obstacle

Ego clouds awareness.

In the dojo, overconfidence blinds the fighter to subtle cues.

In marketing, success blinds brands to emerging threats.

Blockbuster underestimated streaming.

Kodak underestimated digital photography.

They saw the present clearly, but not the shift.

Awareness requires humility.

It demands that we question assumptions.

Listening as Strategic Practice

Awareness in marketing is built through disciplined listening:

- Social listening tools
- Customer feedback loops
- Sales team insights
- Post-campaign debriefs

But listening is not passive.

It is interpretive.

In martial arts, reading breath patterns reveals fatigue.

In marketing, reading customer sentiment reveals unmet needs.

Those who observe deeply move decisively.

The Stillness before Movement

There is a moment in sparring, a stillness before action.

The practitioner assesses distance, timing, and posture.

This pause is not hesitation.

It is preparation.

Marketing requires similar pauses:

Before entering a new channel.

Before repositioning a brand.

Before responding to a competitor.

Speed without awareness creates noise.

Speed with awareness creates impact.

Awareness Builds Adaptability

Adaptability is impossible without awareness.

To flow like water, one must first understand the shape of the container.

Brands that cultivate continuous insight —through data analytics, cultural scanning, and customer empathy—respond with clarity rather than panic.

Awareness reduces surprise.

Reduced surprise increases composure.

Composure sustains advantage.

Awareness as Daily Practice

Awareness is not a one-time audit.

It is a daily discipline.

- Reviewing performance dashboards.
- Observing customer language.
- Noticing small shifts in engagement patterns.

In martial arts, mastery of awareness allows the practitioner to anticipate rather than react.

In marketing, it allows brands to lead rather than follow.

Closing Reflection

Before you master messaging, master observation.

Before you build campaigns, build insight.

Before you strike, see clearly.

Awareness is the quiet foundation beneath every visible success.

It sharpens strategy.

It tempers the ego.

It prevents miscalculation.

In both martial arts and marketing, the first lesson is not how to act.

It is how to notice.

And those who train awareness daily move with precision when it matters most.

Lesson 5: The Opponent is not the Enemy — The Ego is

In most martial arts traditions, the earliest lesson a student learns has nothing to do with throwing a punch or mastering a stance. It is the simple act of bowing.

Not to surrender.

Not to display submission.

But to acknowledge that the real battle is always internal.

A seasoned martial artist does not fear the opponent standing across the mat.

He fears the opponent within — the ego.

Ego blinds, distorts, inflates, and ultimately destroys.

And this lesson, perhaps more than any other, carries profound implications for modern marketing.

Ego Makes the Fighter Reckless — and the Marketer Tone-Deaf

In combat, ego whispers dangerous messages:

"You're better than them."

"You don't need to prepare."

"You can predict their moves."

This false confidence has defeated more fighters than fists ever have.

It leads to:

- drops in awareness,
- underestimating the opponent,
- ignoring warnings,
- refusing to adapt mid-fight,
- emotional decision-making.

Marketers fall victim to the same traps.

- Ego shows up when teams:
- fall in love with their own ideas,
- ignore customer feedback,
- dismiss competitor strategies,
- rely on outdated assumptions,
- copy themselves instead of evolving,
- chase awards instead of outcomes.

In both dojo and boardroom, the ego creates illusions that separate perception from reality.

Competitors are not Enemies — They are Mirrors

Martial artists learn that the person they spar with is not an adversary but a mirror—someone who reveals weaknesses the fighter cannot see alone.

The opponent's strength exposes your imbalance.

Their speed highlights your hesitation.

Their strategy reveals your rigidity.

Marketers benefit from the same perspective.

Competitors are not villains.

They are teachers.

A rival brand can reveal:

- the cracks in your positioning,
- the stagnation in your messaging,
- the gaps in customer experience,
- the complacency in your strategy.

Some of the most successful global brands evolved because competition forced them to confront their blind spots:

- Apple sharpened its brand identity because of Microsoft.
- Dove's Real Beauty movement emerged in response to beauty-industry norms.
- Nike's consistency was forged in the pressure of Adidas and Reebok.

In martial arts, gratitude toward one's opponent is considered a mark of maturity.

In marketing, it is a mark of strategic intelligence.

The Ego Creates Noise — Awareness Creates Clarity

Ego is loud.

Awareness is quiet.

Ego pushes marketers to talk more, claim more, promise more.

Awareness teaches restraint, empathy, and timing.

When ego drives decisions, brands:

- interrupt instead of engage,
- assume instead of listening,
- push content instead of creating value,
- focus on themselves instead of the customer.

Awareness shifts the lens outward.

A master marketer resembles a black-belt fighter — attuned, observant, emotionally regulated, and deeply aware of the energy of the person in front of them.

The most Dangerous Form of Ego: "We Know Our Customer"

Every martial artist knows the fight is lost the moment they assume they "know" what the opponent will do.

The same arrogance cripples brands.

Executives often claim — with great conviction — "We know our customer."

But customer reality evolves:

- attitudes shift,
- expectations rise,
- technologies disrupt habits,
- cultural movements reshape norms.

Ego leads to stagnant personas and outdated assumptions.

Awareness leads to:

- continuous discovery,
- iterative learning,
- fresh insights,
- humility-driven strategy.

Disney, Netflix, Spotify, Tesla — all thrive not on ego but on relentless curiosity.

Ego Protects — Mastery Evolves

The ego's primary function is protection — it shields us from discomfort, uncertainty, and criticism.

But mastery thrives in discomfort.

A martial artist grows not by repeating what he is good at, but by confronting what he is not.

Great marketers do the same.

They:

- embrace negative feedback,
- dissect failed campaigns,
- invite critique,
- seek perspectives outside their silo,
- test assumptions ruthlessly.

In organizations ruled by ego, innovation suffocates.

In organizations ruled by curiosity, innovation compounds.

A Story from the Dojo: The Lesson of the Empty Cup

A classic Zen parable often told in martial arts dojos captures the danger of ego:

A master pours tea into a student's cup but does not stop — the tea overflows.

The student exclaims, "Master, the cup is full!"

The master replies,

"Like this cup, you are full of your own opinions. How can i show you the way unless you first empty your cup?"

In marketing, "emptying the cup" means:

- questioning your assumptions,
- re-evaluating what you believe is true about your brand,
- relearning your customers,
- releasing pride in past successes.

Ego clings.

Mastery lets go.

Brands that Win are the Ones that Bow

The bow — one of the most recognizable gestures in martial arts — symbolizes humility, respect, and readiness to learn.

Brands that "bow" metaphorically succeed because they:

- listen before speaking,
- study before acting,
- adapt before breaking,
- acknowledge customer power,
- revere the craft of marketing.

In an era of algorithmic arrogance and loud digital noise, humility becomes a competitive advantage.

The Paradox: Overcoming Ego makes you Unbeatable

The great martial artists — Musashi, Bruce Lee, Morihei Ueshiba — repeatedly taught that humility is what makes a fighter truly formidable.

Similarly, the brands with the greatest "soft power" — Apple, Patagonia, Airbnb, Nike — built influence by mastering awareness rather than aggression.

Ego is brittle.

Awareness is fluid.

Ego inflates.

Awareness illuminates.

The marketer who defeats the ego becomes adaptable, creative, resilient, and deeply connected to customer truth.

In that state, there is no opponent — only opportunity.

Closing Insight: The Real Competitor Lives Within

The martial artist rises every morning not to fight others, but to fight the part of themselves that resists growth.

The marketer, too, must confront:

- the ego that refuses feedback,
- the pride that clings to old campaigns,
- the fear of being wrong,
- the illusion of certainty.

This inner battle determines the outer results.

And when the ego is defeated, mastery becomes possible.

In martial arts and marketing alike:

The most dangerous opponent is not across the mat. It is within your mind.

Lesson 6: Repetition Builds Instinct — The "Marketing Kata"

Every martial arts tradition has kata — structured sequences practiced over and over until the body moves without hesitation and the mind becomes quiet. To an outsider, kata may appear repetitive or even monotonous. But to the practitioner, each repetition is a step toward mastery.

Martial artists know something marketers often forget:

Repetition is not redundancy — it is refinement.

In marketing, the "kata" is the disciplined repetition of strategic practice:

- revisiting customer insights,
- refining positioning,
- testing variations of a message,
- iterating on creative concepts,
- reviewing performance data,
- improving process rituals.

Mastery emerges not from doing many things once, but from doing the most important things again and again with increasing precision.

This is why great brands have a signature rhythm — a consistency built on well-rehearsed frameworks. Nike's relentless refinement of its motivational storytelling, Apple's iterative simplicity, and Coca-Cola's brand rituals all reflect kata-like discipline.

The novice marketer searches for excitement in novelty.

The master marketer finds depth in repetition.

Lesson 7: Strength Comes from Centeredness, Not Force

Ask any martial artist where real power comes from, and they will never say "the arms." They will say:

"From the center."

From grounding.

From alignment.

From core stability.

Force without balance is dangerous — to both the opponent and the practitioner.

Marketing operates the same way. When brands chase trends, react impulsively, or try to shout louder than the competition, they expend enormous energy but achieve little impact.

Centeredness in marketing means being anchored in:

- your brand purpose,
- your values,
- your authentic voice,
- your core promise,
- your strategic north star.

A well-centered brand does not need to push itself onto customers; it pulls them by its clarity and resonance.

Think Patagonia, whose environmental stance grounds every message. Or Dove, whose purpose-centered platform anchors decades of campaigns.

Force creates resistance.

Centeredness creates influence.

Lesson 8: Failure is Feedback — Sparring, Not Defeat

In the dojo, you are expected to fall.

You are expected to be thrown.

You are expected to misjudge distance, timing, and balance.

These failures are not punishments — they are feedback loops.

Sparring is not about winning; it is about learning.

Marketing desperately needs this mindset.

Campaigns will miss.

Customer journeys will reveal unexpected friction points.

Positioning statements may fail to resonate.

Innovations may arrive before the market is ready.

Brilliant marketers treat these moments as sparring sessions — temporary, necessary, and deeply instructive.

The data behind a failed idea is not an indictment; it is intelligence.

The worst mistake a marketer can make is to interpret failure as defeat.

The best mistake a marketer can make is one that leads to adaptation.

Just as martial artists bow to each other before sparring, marketers must bow to their failures — with gratitude for the lessons they bring.

Lesson 9: Mastery Requires Humility and Lifelong Learning

"The more you know, the more you realize you don't know."

This ancient martial insight reflects a universal truth: the higher one climbs, the more humility is required.

At the highest levels of martial arts, humility is not politeness — it is a survival skill. The arrogant fighter stops learning. The humble fighter evolves continuously.

Marketing demands the same disposition.

The landscape shifts constantly:

- new technologies,
- new consumer expectations,
- new platforms,
- new competitors,
- new cultural signals.

Marketers who believe they have "figured it out" become obsolete faster than they expect.

Humility keeps curiosity alive.

Curiosity keeps strategy fresh.

Fresh strategy keeps brands relevant.

This "beginner's mind" — shoshin in Zen tradition — is the antidote to stagnation.

It encourages marketers to ask questions even when they think they know the answers. It reminds leaders that every campaign is an experiment, not a certainty.

In marketing, as in martial arts: The moment you stop learning is the moment you stop leading.

Lesson 10: True Victory is Inner — not against Others

Martial arts teaches that the greatest victory is not defeating another person but mastering one's own mind.

The real fight is not external — it is internal.

Against fear.

Against doubt.

Against ego.

Against complacency.

Modern marketing glorifies competition — battle metaphors, market wars, "crushing" competitors. Yet the brands that truly dominate do not obsess over rivals. They obsess over improving themselves.

True victory in marketing is not:

- higher volume of ads,
- louder messaging,
- bigger budgets,
- or even market share.

True victory is:

- earning trust,
- building loyalty,
- delivering meaningful value,
- creating emotional resonance,
- remaining relevant for decades.

The martial artist learns that victory achieved through aggression fades quickly. But victory earned through mastery endures.

In the same way, a brand that wins through manipulation or noise may see short-term gains — but a brand that wins through integrity, mastery, and customer understanding earns a legacy.

The real competitor is not another brand.

It is the older version of your own brand.

Winning means becoming better than you were yesterday.

Ten Lessons Marketers can Learn from Martial Arts

The Dojo Principles of Strategy, Discipline & Mastery

1. **Mastery Takes Time**

   Marketing success—like a black belt—comes only through sustained, consistent practice.

2. **Discipline is Essential**

   Great campaigns require commitment, repetition, and rigorous attention to detail.

3. **Know your Competition**

   Study your rivals 'strengths, weaknesses, and patterns before making your move.

4. **Adapt to Change**

   Markets shift. Channels evolve. Flexibility is a strategic advantage.

5. **The Opponent is not the Enemy—the Ego is**

   Remove ego, defensiveness, and assumption. Clear thinking wins.

6. **Understand your Capabilities**

   Identify and strengthen your unique value—your "signature technique."

7. **Mind and Body are Connected**

   Great marketers manage energy, focus, and mental clarity under pressure.

8. **Defense is as Important as Offense**

   Brand resilience, reputation, and customer trust protect long-term success.

9. **Grit Leads to Growth**

   Every setback is a sparring lesson that sharpens skill and resilience.

10. **Practice Humility**

    Stay teachable. Listen deeply. Continuous learning is the true path to mastery.

12 Real-World Case Studies

Case Study #1. Apple: The Minimalist "Zen Strike" Communication Model

In martial arts, the most powerful strike is often the simplest one.

There is no wasted motion.

No unnecessary flourish.

No excess energy.

Just clarity. Precision. Timing.

Few companies embody this principle in modern marketing more consistently than Apple.

Apple's communication strategy can be described as a "Zen Strike" model — a minimalist, high-impact approach rooted in restraint, focus, and disciplined subtraction. Where competitors shout, Apple pauses. Where others crowd their messaging with features, Apple reduces it to essence.

And in that reduction, power emerges.

1. **The Principle of Subtraction**

   In many martial traditions — particularly those influenced by Zen philosophy — mastery is not about accumulation. It is about elimination.

   Remove the unnecessary.

   Retain the essential.

   Apple's communication mirrors this discipline:

   - Sparse product slides
   - Minimal copy
   - White space as a strategic tool
   - Focus on one core idea per campaign

   Think of the early iPod campaigns.

   One silhouette.

   One color background.

One message: "1,000 songs in your pocket."

No technical clutter.

No processor speeds.

No specification overload.

This is not accidental minimalism.

It is trained minimalism.

In dojo terms: this is kata refined to its purest form.

2. **Focus: One Strike at a Time**

A novice throws many uncontrolled punches.

A master chooses one and lands it.

Apple's keynote presentations are masterclasses in focused communication.

When Steve Jobs introduced the iPhone in 2007, he did not overwhelm the audience with feature lists. He framed the narrative around three simple ideas:

- A widescreen iPod
- A revolutionary phone
- A breakthrough internet communicator

Then he revealed they were one device.

That moment was not just a product unveiling.

It was strategic choreography.

A Zen Strike.

The communication principle at work: Control the narrative by narrowing the lens.

Marketers often dilute impact by trying to communicate everything.

Apple communicates one idea with total conviction.

3. **Silence as Strategy**

In martial arts, stillness is not weakness.

It is readiness.

Apple understands silence.

- Long pauses in keynote presentations
- Slow, cinematic product videos

- Clean, uncluttered web layouts
- Sparse retail spaces

Silence creates tension.

Tension creates attention.

Attention creates desire.

In marketing terms, this is the disciplined management of cognitive load.

Research in behavioral science shows that simplicity increases perceived value and reduces decision fatigue. Apple leverages this. The brand's aesthetic reduces friction and invites focus.

Their communication does not fight for attention.

It commands it.

4. **The Power of the Essential Narrative**

Many brands describe what their product does.

Apple describes what the product means.

This reflects a deeper martial principle:

Technique is secondary to intent.

From "Think Different" to "Shot on iPhone," Apple communicates identity, aspiration, and creative empowerment.

This is strategic positioning at its purest form.

The Zen Strike model rests on three pillars:

1. Clarity of Purpose
2. Reduction to Essence
3. Confidence in Delivery

There is no defensive over-explaining.

No anxious justification.

Just a clear strike.

5. **Design as Discipline**

Minimalism is not decoration.

It is discipline.

Apple's visual consistency — typography, layout, product photography, retail architecture — reflects an internal dojo of design governance.

This is not an aesthetic preference.

It is strategic repetition.

Every touchpoint reinforces the same values:

- Precision
- Simplicity
- Craftsmanship
- Control

In martial training, repetition builds instinct.

In branding, repetition builds trust.

6. **What Marketers can Learn**

The Zen Strike model offers several dojo lessons:

1. *Eliminate before you Add*: Before increasing content, ask: What can be removed?
2. *Communicate One Core Idea*: If everything is important, nothing is.
3. *Use Silence Strategically*: White space and restraint increase perceived sophistication.
4. *Trust Simplicity*: Complex markets do not require complex communication.
5. *Align Design with Identity*: Minimalism must reflect internal discipline, not superficial styling.

7. **The Risk of False Minimalism**

However, there is a caution.

Minimalism without substance is emptiness.

A strike without training is ineffective.

Apple's simplicity works because it is backed by:

- Product integration
- Ecosystem coherence
- Supply chain discipline
- Brand consistency

Minimalist communication only succeeds when the underlying value proposition is strong.

In martial arts, form without strength collapses under pressure.

8. **The Zen Strike as a Competitive Advantage**

   In crowded categories, most brands increase noise.

   Apple reduces it.

   Where competitors release comparison charts, Apple releases a single image.

   Where others explain, Apple demonstrates.

   Where others argue, Apple reveals.

   The result is psychological dominance, not through aggression, but through composure.

   That is the essence of the Zen Strike.

Closing Reflection

A master does not win by overpowering every opponent.

A master wins by choosing the right moment, the right technique, and executing them without hesitation.

Apple's communication model teaches marketers that clarity, restraint, and disciplined focus are not weaknesses.

They are weapons.

And in a marketplace saturated with noise, the most powerful message is often the one delivered with the fewest words.

Case Study #2. Coca-Cola vs. Pepsi: Brand Rivalry as Philosophical Sparring — Lessons in Humility and Identity

In martial arts, sparring is not combat.

It is dialogue.

Two practitioners meet — not to destroy each other — but to test their skills, sharpen their awareness, and reveal weaknesses. The opponent becomes the teacher.

Few brand rivalries illustrate this dynamic more vividly than the enduring contest between Coca-Cola and PepsiCo.

For over a century, their rivalry has been less about sugar water and more about identity.

Tradition versus rebellion.

Continuity versus disruption.

Heritage versus youth.

This is not merely market competition.

It is philosophical sparring.

1. **The Dojo of Identity**

   In martial arts, one must know one's style.

   A karate practitioner does not suddenly become a judo master mid-fight.

   A disciplined fighter respects lineage.

   Coca-Cola has long embodied stability, nostalgia, and timelessness. Since its late-19th-century origins, it has positioned itself as the drink of shared moments—family gatherings, global events, and holiday rituals. Its iconic red script and Santa Claus campaigns reinforced emotional continuity.

   Pepsi, by contrast, has historically chosen the counter-position. Youthful. Energetic. Disruptive. It leaned into cultural shifts — music, pop icons, generational change.

Their rivalry thus became a battle of archetypes:

- Coca-Cola: The Master — calm, rooted, enduring.
- Pepsi: The Challenger — agile, provocative, adaptive.

In dojo terms: one anchored in stance; the other probing for openings.

2. **The Pepsi Challenge: The Aggressive Strike**

   In the 1970s, Pepsi launched the now-famous "Pepsi Challenge," a blind taste test that suggested consumers preferred Pepsi's sweeter profile.

   This was not merely a marketing tactic.

   It was a strategic strike.

   Instead of confronting Coca-Cola's emotional positioning, Pepsi attacked the product directly: taste.

   In sparring, this resembles a challenger targeting a perceived vulnerability. If Coca-Cola's strength was heritage, Pepsi sought to reframe the fight around immediacy.

   The campaign forced Coca-Cola to respond.

   And here the martial lesson deepens.

3. **The "New Coke" Moment: When Ego Enters the Mat**

   In 1985, Coca-Cola reformulated its flagship product in response to competitive pressure and blind taste test results. The introduction of "New Coke" is now studied as one of the most significant marketing missteps in modern business history.

   But from a martial perspective, it is not merely a mistake.

   It is a lesson in humility.

   Coca-Cola had allowed the arena of sparring to redefine its identity. In reacting to Pepsi's strike, it momentarily abandoned its deeper philosophy.

   A seasoned martial artist knows: Never let the opponent dictate your stance.

   Consumers reacted strongly. The backlash was swift. Within months, Coca-Cola restored its original formula as "Coca-Cola Classic."

   Here lies the profound lesson:

   The true error was not experimentation.

   It was forgetting what the brand represented.

Yet the recovery demonstrated mastery.

Coca-Cola listened.

Adjusted.

Returned to the center.

In martial arts, this is called regaining balance after a destabilizing move.

Humility restored equilibrium.

4. **Pepsi's Fluid Identity: Agility as Strategy**

   While Coca-Cola leaned into tradition, Pepsi leaned into evolution.

   From partnerships with Michael Jackson and Britney Spears to decades-long pop culture integrations, Pepsi positioned itself as the beverage of "now."

   This agility mirrors a different martial principle: adaptability.

   If Coca-Cola resembles a rooted stance, Pepsi resembles a more fluid fighting style — shifting, experimenting, aligning with cultural momentum.

   But agility carries its own risk.

   Without a stable center, movement can become drift.

   Over the decades, Pepsi has periodically struggled to define its brand — oscillating between youth rebellion, celebrity glamour, and lifestyle branding.

   In dojo language: speed must be anchored in philosophy.

5. **Sparring without Hatred**

   One of the most remarkable aspects of this rivalry is its theatrical quality.

   Both brands have occasionally referenced each other in advertising — playful jabs rather than hostile attacks. The rivalry became part of their shared narrative ecosystem.

   In martial arts, sparring partners often bow before and after engagement.

   Respect underlies competition.

   Coca-Cola and Pepsi have shaped one another's evolution. Each forced the other to sharpen its messaging, innovate its packaging, and refine its positioning.

   The "opponent" became a co-creator of excellence.

6. **Lessons in Humility**

   This case offers several dojo lessons:

   1. *Do not Confuse Data with Identity:* Blind taste tests revealed preference. But preference does not equal brand meaning.
   2. *Reaction without Reflection is Dangerous:* Strategic decisions made under competitive pressure can distort long-term positioning.
   3. *Humility Enables Recovery:* Coca-Cola's willingness to reverse course preserved trust.
   4. *Agility Requires Anchor:* Pepsi's flexibility works best when grounded in clear philosophical positioning.
   5. *Rivalry Sharpens Skill:* Competition is not hostility. It is refinement.

7. **Identity Over Tactics**

   In martial arts, techniques evolve. Philosophy endures.

   Coca-Cola's strength lies in emotional continuity — "Open Happiness," "Share a Coke," and global unity campaigns.

   Pepsi's strength lies in cultural alignment— its connection to music, sports, and youth identity.

   The rivalry illustrates that brands must choose their philosophical stance before choosing tactics.

   Otherwise, sparring becomes chaos.

8. **The Deeper Teaching**

   The Coca-Cola vs. Pepsi rivalry reveals something deeper about marketing:

   Markets are arenas of meaning, not just transactions.

   Brands compete not merely for shelf space, but for symbolic territory.

   One claims tradition.

   The other claims change.

   One bows to heritage.

   The other bows to momentum.

   In the dojo of the marketplace, both styles can succeed — if practiced with awareness.

Closing Reflection

In sparring, the goal is not to eliminate the opponent.

It is to elevate oneself.

Coca-Cola and Pepsi demonstrate that rivalry can expose ego, test identity, and demand humility. But when approached with discipline, rivalry becomes refinement.

The true mastery lies not in defeating the opponent, but in remaining true to your stance while adapting with grace.

And in that balance between humility and identity, brands find their center.

Case Study #3. Dove: The "Real Beauty" Campaign — Authentic Storytelling as Courage and Ethical Redefinition

In martial arts, there comes a moment when the practitioner must decide:

Will I imitate the dominant style?

Or will I redefine the form?

In 2004, Dove chose the latter.

At a time when the global beauty industry was saturated with perfected images, digitally altered ideals, and aspirational distance, Dove executed what can only be described as a disciplined, ethical strike.

Not louder.

Not flashier.

But braver.

The "Real Beauty" campaign was not simply a marketing initiative.

It was a philosophical repositioning.

And like any true martial innovation, it required courage.

1. **The Traditional Form: Beauty as Aspiration**

   For decades, beauty advertising operated within a predictable kata:

   - Idealized bodies
   - Flawless skin
   - Youth as virtue
   - Perfection as promise

   Brands sold aspiration through exclusion.

   Beauty was rare.

   Beauty was distant.

   Beauty was unattainable.

   This approach was commercially effective, but philosophically narrow.

   The industry sparred under the same set of rules.

2. **The Ethical Pivot: Redefining the Arena**

   Dove stepped back and asked a deeper question:

   What if the problem is not the consumer's insecurity, but the definition of beauty itself?

   The "Real Beauty" campaign introduced:

   Women of diverse shapes, sizes, and ages

   - Minimal retouching
   - Emotional storytelling
   - Conversations around self-esteem

   This was not merely a creative pivot.

   It was ethical reframing.

   In martial arts, this resembles changing the arena rather than escalating force.

   Instead of competing with unrealistic standards, Dove questioned the standards themselves.

   This is strategic courage.

3. **Authentic Storytelling as a Discipline**

   Authenticity is not spontaneity.

   It is disciplined truth-telling.

   The campaign's storytelling approach focused on lived experiences:

   - Women describing their insecurities
   - Mothers speaking about daughters
   - Sketch experiments revealing self-perception bias

   One of the most widely discussed executions — the "Real Beauty Sketches" film — demonstrated that women described themselves more critically than strangers did.

   The lesson was not aesthetic.

   It was psychological.

   In dojo language: Dove shifted from external appearance to internal perception.

   They moved from surface technique to inner philosophy.

4. **Courage in Brand Positioning**

   Redefining beauty is not safe.

   It risks backlash.

   It risks accusations of opportunism.

   It risks alienating traditional expectations.

   Courage in martial arts is not recklessness.

   It is a controlled conviction.

   Dove sustained the "Real Beauty" platform over the years, not as a single campaign burst, but as an evolving commitment. They expanded the effort to include educational programs on self-esteem and body confidence.

   This sustained discipline distinguished philosophy from stunt.

   The campaign became a stance.

5. **The Paradox of Imperfection**

   Here lies a subtle insight.

   Dove sells soap, not ideology.

   The campaign did not abandon commercial objectives. Instead, it aligned commercial intent with emotional truth.

   In martial arts, strength often emerges from acceptance of limitation.

   Flexibility emerges from acknowledging rigidity.

   By embracing imperfection, Dove increased relatability.

   By increasing relatability, it strengthened trust.

   By strengthening trust, it increased brand equity.

   Courage and commerce aligned.

6. **Ethical Redefinition as Competitive Strategy**

   The beauty category is crowded. Functional differentiation is minimal. Moisturizing formulas can be replicated.

   Ethical positioning is harder to copy.

   Dove's redefinition of beauty became a strategic moat.

   Other brands attempted to be inclusive, but few sustained it with equal depth.

   The lesson: Philosophical differentiation outlasts tactical differentiation.

   In sparring terms, Dove did not simply counterpunch competitors.

   It altered the rhythm of the match.

7. The Risk of Inconsistency

Yet mastery requires vigilance.

Critics have pointed out tensions within the parent company, Unilever, which owns other beauty brands that sometimes adhere to traditional beauty ideals.

This highlights an important dojo truth: Integrity must be systemic, not episodic.

Authenticity is fragile.

If action and messaging diverge, the strike loses force.

Dove's long-term challenge remains alignment across portfolio and practice.

8. Lessons for Marketers

The Real Beauty campaign teaches several martial principles:

1. *Redefine the Arena*: Do not merely compete within existing rules — question them.
2. *Authenticity Requires Discipline*: Consistency over time proves sincerity.
3. *Courage Creates Distinction*: Bold ethical positioning sets brands apart from the noise.
4. *Emotional Truth Outlasts Feature Claims*: Functional benefits fade. Identity persists.
5. *Integrity must Extend beyond Messaging*: The philosophy must match the ecosystem.

9. Beauty as Inner Strength

In martial traditions, the most advanced practitioners display quiet strength.

No theatrics.

No exaggeration.

Just presence.

Dove's campaign did something rare: It replaced idealized beauty with dignified presence.

The brand bowed not to perfection, but to reality.

And in that bow, it found power.

Closing Reflection

The Real Beauty campaign was not a loud strike.

It was a principled stance.

It required the courage to reject dominant conventions and the humility to center real human stories.

In the dojo of marketing, courage without discipline collapses.

Discipline without courage stagnates.

Dove demonstrated that when authenticity and conviction align, a brand does not merely sell products; it reshapes perception.

And in reshaping perception, it changes the form of the fight itself.

Case Study #4. Garage Beer: The "Brewmite" Campaign — Storytelling as a Martial Art of Simplicity

In martial arts, the most powerful technique is often the smallest.

A subtle wrist turn.

A precise shift of weight.

A strike delivered without flourish.

Garage Beer's "Brewmite" campaign demonstrates this principle in modern brand storytelling.

In a marketplace crowded with craft-beer complexity — flavor notes, hops taxonomy, artisanal credentials, elaborate origin myths — Garage Beer chose a radically disciplined path.

It did not escalate.

It simplified.

And in that simplification, it differentiated.

1. **The Overcrowded Dojo of Craft Beer**

   The craft beer industry often behaves like a dojo full of ambitious novices — each trying to prove mastery through elaboration.

   - Exotic ingredients
   - Intricate brewing processes
   - Clever but dense label design
   - Hyper-descriptive tasting notes

   This approach signals sophistication. But it also increases cognitive load.

   Consumers faced with too many choices often retreat to familiarity.

   Garage Beer understood this tension.

   Instead of adding technique, it removed it.

2. **The Brewmite Concept: A Micro-Strike**

   The "Brewmite" campaign centered on a simple, humorous idea: a tiny mascot-like character embodying the beer's identity — playful, uncomplicated, unpretentious.

The storytelling was lean.

The visuals were clean.

The messaging was clear.

No excessive claims.

No craft snobbery.

No complexity theater.

In martial terms, this was a low, controlled strike — delivered at the right moment.

The Brewmite did not overwhelm.

It charmed.

3. **Simplicity as Strategic Discipline**

Simplicity is not laziness.

It is discipline.

Garage Beer's positioning emphasized:

- Easy drinking
- Approachability
- Social enjoyment
- A return to uncomplicated beer culture

Where competitors marketed intensity and flavor extremity, Garage Beer marketed ease.

This resembles a martial artist who avoids unnecessary movements, conserving energy and controlling tempo.

The Brewmite became a symbol of this restraint.

4. **Humor as Soft Power**

In sparring, not every technique is forceful. Some disarm through redirection.

Humor functions this way in marketing.

The Brewmite campaign used lightness to contrast with the seriousness of craft-beer narratives. By not taking itself too seriously, the brand created emotional accessibility.

This is a lesson in tonal discipline.

Intensity is common.

Warmth is rare.

And rarity attracts attention.

5. **Storytelling as Kata**

   In martial arts, kata is a set of movements practiced repeatedly until they become instinctive.

   Garage Beer's storytelling maintained consistency:

   - Simple character
   - Consistent tone
   - Clean packaging
   - Minimalist communication

   Repetition builds recognition.

   Recognition builds trust.

   Trust builds brand equity.

   The Brewmite was not a one-off gimmick. It functioned as a narrative anchor.

6. **The Power of Contrast**

   Every dojo has dominant styles. Differentiation often comes not from superiority, but from contrast.

   Garage Beer did not try to out-craft the craft brewers.

   It positioned itself as an antidote.

   This is a profound marketing lesson: You do not always win by escalating complexity.

   Sometimes you win by restoring simplicity.

   In martial terms: when opponents move wildly, stillness becomes strategic advantage.

7. **Identity through Restraint**

   The Brewmite campaign reflects a deeper philosophy: identity through subtraction.

   Instead of:

   "We are more artisanal."

   "We are more innovative."

   "We are more premium."

Garage Beer implicitly said:

"We are less complicated."

That restraint creates clarity.

Clarity reduces friction.

Reduced friction increases purchase probability.

Behavioral science supports this. Consumers often choose options that feel cognitively lighter.

Garage Beer built cognitive lightness into its brand DNA.

8. Discipline as Differentiator

The real lesson is not humor.

It is restraint.

Many brands can be clever.

Few can remain simple.

Remaining simple in a noisy environment requires conviction.

It requires saying no — to feature overload, to identity drift, to creative overreach.

In martial arts, discipline separates hobbyists from masters.

Garage Beer's Brewmite campaign demonstrates how disciplined storytelling can create space in a saturated category.

9. Lessons for Marketers

From this case, marketers can learn:

1. *Simplicity is a Competitive Strategy*: Subtraction can differentiate more than addition.
2. *Character Builds Memory*: A simple mascot can anchor brand identity.
3. *Humor Reduces Defensive Resistance*: Light tone increases approachability.
4. *Cognitive Ease Drives Choice*: Less friction often leads to greater adoption.
5. *Discipline Sustains Differentiation*: Consistency outperforms novelty.

Closing Reflection

In martial arts, mastery is not measured by the number of techniques known.

It is measured by how few are needed.

Garage Beer's Brewmite campaign shows that storytelling does not require epic narratives or complex mythology.

Sometimes, a small character, a simple message, and disciplined repetition are enough.

In a market crowded with noise, simplicity becomes the sharpest strike.

Case Study #5. Netflix: Adaptability and Foresight — Streaming Evolution as Strategic Fluidity

In martial arts, rigidity is defeat.

The stiff fighter breaks.

The fluid fighter survives.

Few companies illustrate this principle of strategic fluidity more clearly than Netflix.

Its journey — from DVD-by-mail startup to global streaming platform to original-content powerhouse — is not simply a story of technological evolution. It is a case study in adaptability, foresight, and disciplined reinvention.

Netflix did not cling to form.

It changed form.

And in doing so, it embodied the martial philosophy famously articulated by Bruce Lee:

"Be like water."

1. **The First Stance: DVD-by-Mail**

   When Netflix was founded in 1997 by Reed Hastings and Marc Randolph, it entered a market dominated by brick-and-mortar rental chains, most notably Blockbuster.

   Blockbuster's model was physical, retail-driven, and late-fee dependent.

   Netflix's model was different:

   - Mail-based distribution
   - Subscription pricing
   - No late fees

   This was the first strategic shift in stance — less about technological superiority, more about customer pain-point awareness.

   In martial terms, Netflix identified the opponent's vulnerability: friction.

   Late fees created resentment.

Physical returns created inconvenience.

Netflix reduced friction.

That reduction was its first strike.

2. **The Decision to Disrupt Itself**

   The deeper lesson emerged not in Netflix's early success, but in its willingness to cannibalize its own model.

   By the mid-2000s, broadband internet adoption was accelerating. Streaming technology was improving.

   Netflix faced a critical question:

   Protect the DVD business?

   Or pivot before the market forces it?

   In 2007, Netflix launched streaming.

   This was not incremental innovation.

   It was strategic self-disruption.

   In martial arts, this is akin to abandoning a familiar stance mid-fight when the terrain changes.

   The novice clings to what works.

   The master adapts before necessity becomes desperation.

   Netflix chose foresight over comfort.

3. **Fluidity as Strategic Philosophy**

   Fluidity requires anticipation.

   Streaming was not yet dominant when Netflix committed to it. Infrastructure was imperfect. Consumer habits were still evolving.

   Yet the leadership recognized an emerging pattern: digital distribution would reshape entertainment consumption.

   Strategic foresight is not prediction.

   It is pattern recognition disciplined by courage.

   Blockbuster, by contrast, hesitated. It treated streaming as an add-on rather than a transformation.

   In sparring terms, one fighter sensed the shift in rhythm. The other did not.

   The result is now a business-school case study in strategic inertia.

4. **From Distributor to Creator**

   Adaptability did not stop at streaming.

   As studios began reclaiming content rights to launch their own platforms, Netflix faced a new threat: dependency.

   If content suppliers become competitors, what is your stance?

   Netflix responded by investing heavily in original programming.

   Shows like House of Cards, Stranger Things, and global-language productions shifted Netflix from distributor to creator.

   This was another self-reinvention.

   Each transformation required disciplined risk-taking:

   - Large capital investments
   - Algorithmic data insights guiding production
   - Global content diversification

   In martial arts, advanced practitioners often develop hybrid styles.

   Netflix evolved into a mixed martial strategy — combining:

   - Technology platform
   - Content studio
   - Data analytics engine
   - Global brand

   Fluid, but structured.

5. **Data as Sensory Awareness**

   A master martial artist reads micro-signals: weight shifts, breath patterns, muscle tension.

   Netflix reads data.

   Viewing habits, pause patterns, genre preferences, completion rates — these insights informed programming decisions and personalization algorithms.

   But data alone is not strategy.

   Data must serve vision.

   Netflix used behavioral insight to enhance user experience, reduce friction, and increase engagement.

   This is technological awareness aligned with strategic intention.

6. **The Cost of Overreach**

   Fluidity carries risk.

   In recent years, Netflix has faced intensified competition from Disney+, Amazon Prime Video, and others.

   Subscriber growth volatility, pricing adjustments, and content saturation have tested the company's resilience.

   Fluidity without discipline can become diffusion.

   The martial lesson here is balance.

   Adaptation must be purposeful, not reactive.

7. **Global Expansion as Expanding the Dojo**

   One of Netflix's most sophisticated adaptations was its embrace of global content.

   Rather than exporting American programming alone, Netflix invested in local-language productions — from South Korea to Spain to India.

   This approach:

   - Reduced cultural friction
   - Increased regional relevance
   - Created global cross-pollination of hits

   Fluidity here meant respecting terrain.

   In martial arts, fighting styles adapt to the environment—open space, confined quarters, uneven ground.

   Netflix understood that global markets required contextual adaptation, not uniform export.

8. **Lessons in Strategic Fluidity**

   From Netflix's evolution, marketers can draw profound dojo lessons:

   1. *Anticipate Terrain Shifts*: Do not wait for the ground to move beneath you.
   2. *Be Willing to Cannibalize Yourself*: Better to disrupt your own model than be disrupted by others.
   3. *Align Data with Vision*: Insight without philosophy becomes noise.
   4. *Build Hybrid Strength*: Combine capabilities — technology, creativity, analytics.

5. *Adapt without Losing Core Identity*: Fluidity must still be anchored in purpose.

9. Foresight as a Discipline

The romantic narrative of Netflix celebrates bold pivots.

But behind each pivot was disciplined leadership, scenario planning, and a willingness to endure short-term criticism for long-term positioning.

Adaptability is not improvisation.

It is trained responsiveness.

Like water, Netflix changed shape — from DVD envelopes to streaming interfaces to an original content platform — while maintaining its underlying flow: convenient, on-demand entertainment.

Closing Reflection

In martial arts, the practitioner who survives longest is not the strongest.

It is the one who adapts.

Netflix's journey demonstrates that strategic fluidity — grounded in foresight and disciplined reinvention — is a powerful competitive advantage.

Markets shift.

Technology evolves.

Competitors emerge.

But the brand that flows without losing center does not merely react.

It shapes the current.

And in shaping the current, it writes the future of the arena itself.

Case Study #6: Nike: Discipline in Message and Purpose — Mastery through Repetition and Consistency

In martial arts, a master does not practice thousands of techniques at once.

The master practices one technique thousands of times.

Repetition builds instinct.

Consistency builds identity.

Few brands embody this discipline of message more powerfully than Nike.

From its founding vision to its modern global presence, Nike has demonstrated a singular commitment to purpose-driven storytelling — a focus so disciplined that it resembles kata practice in the dojo.

1. **The Core Stance: "Just Do It."**

   In 1988, Nike introduced a line that would become one of the most enduring slogans in marketing history:

   "Just Do It."

   It was simple.

   It was direct.

   It was uncompromising.

   Over decades, this phrase has remained central — not as decoration, but as philosophy.

   Many brands refresh slogans frequently, chasing novelty.

   Nike returned to its mantra, again and again.

   In martial terms, this is not stagnation.

   It is refinement.

   Each campaign became a variation of the same foundational kata:

   - Push beyond limits
   - Confront doubt
   - Embrace challenge
   - Act decisively

   The repetition created resonance.

2. **Message Discipline Over Tactical Noise**

   The sportswear category is crowded:

   - Performance claims
   - Fabric technology
   - Cushioning innovation
   - Design trends

   Nike participates in product innovation, but its communication rarely leads with features.

   Instead, Nike leads with belief.

   From Michael Jordan to Serena Williams, from Colin Kaepernick to everyday runners, Nike consistently frames sport as a metaphor for human potential.

   This is disciplined positioning.

   Nike does not fight on every battlefield.

   It fights on the battlefield of inspiration.

3. **Consistency across Decades**

   One of the defining marks of mastery is continuity.

   Campaigns evolve. Athletes change. Cultural contexts shift. Yet Nike's narrative spine remains intact:

   - The underdog rises.
   - The doubter is defeated.
   - The impossible is challenged.

   Consider the 2018 campaign featuring Colin Kaepernick.

   Nike risked controversy by aligning with a polarizing athlete and a broader social issue. Yet the campaign was not a departure from brand philosophy — it was an extension of it.

   "Believe in something. Even if it means sacrificing everything."

   That is "Just Do It" expressed in another register.

   Discipline means remaining faithful to purpose, even under pressure.

4. **Repetition as Brand Strength Training**

   In martial arts, repetition builds muscle memory.

   In branding, repetition builds mental memory.

Nike's visual and verbal consistency includes:

- The Swoosh
- Bold typography
- Minimal copy
- High-contrast photography
- Focus on the athlete's expression

The Swoosh is rarely altered.

The tone rarely softens.

This disciplined repetition strengthens recall and emotional association.

Where many brands experiment widely, Nike refines deeply.

5. **Emotional Conditioning**

Nike's campaigns function as psychological training sessions.

They do not simply display athletes performing.

They frame effort as identity.

In dojo terms, Nike trains its audience to think like practitioners:

- Embrace pain as growth
- Reject excuses
- Act despite fear

The brand does not promise comfort.

It promises transformation.

This emotional conditioning builds loyalty that transcends product.

6. **Purpose as Anchor**

Nike's mission — "to bring inspiration and innovation to every athlete in the world" — contains a radical clause:

"If you have a body, you are an athlete."

That philosophical expansion of identity mirrors a martial principle:

Every person has potential.

By redefining who qualifies as an athlete, Nike expanded its arena.

This is not opportunistic marketing.

It is disciplined inclusion aligned with purpose.

7. **Courage within Consistency**

   Consistency does not mean predictability.

   Nike has taken bold stances — from gender equity to racial justice — yet these positions align with its core narrative of empowerment and defiance.

   Courage without alignment is chaos.

   Alignment without courage is stagnation.

   Nike balances both.

   In sparring terms, it maintains a stance while adjusting technique.

8. **Lessons for Marketers**

   From Nike's disciplined messaging, several dojo lessons emerge:

   1. *Master the Core Idea*: One powerful idea, repeated consistently, outweighs many fragmented messages.
   2. *Align Purpose with Action*: Messaging must reflect authentic conviction.
   3. *Repetition Builds Equity*: Brand memory compounds over time.
   4. *Discipline Beats Novelty*: Consistency creates psychological ownership.
   5. *Expand Identity Carefully*: Redefine your category without abandoning your foundation.

9. **The Power of Relentless Focus**

   The temptation in marketing is to chase trends.

   The temptation in martial arts is to learn every style.

   Masters resist both impulses.

   Nike's genius lies not in constant reinvention, but in disciplined amplification.

   The Swoosh, the mantra, the defiant tone — repeated, refined, reinforced.

   Over time, this repetition became cultural memory.

Closing Reflection

In the dojo, mastery is quiet.

It is built through thousands of disciplined movements no one sees.

Nike's marketing mastery rests not on isolated creative brilliance, but on relentless adherence to purpose.

While others pivot slogans and chase novelty, Nike returns to its stance:

Just do it.

And in that disciplined repetition, the brand does not merely advertise.

It trains.

Case Study #7: Oreo: "Dunk in the Dark" — Tactical Adaptability and the "Be Water" Philosophy in Real-Time Marketing

In martial arts, speed alone does not win.

Awareness does.

The practitioner who senses a shift in rhythm — and responds without hesitation — often prevails.

On February 3, 2013, during Super Bowl XLVII, a power outage plunged the stadium into darkness for 34 minutes. Millions of viewers watched the interruption unfold live.

Most brands paused.

Oreo did not.

Within minutes, Oreo's social media team posted a simple image with a single line:

"You can still dunk in the dark."

The tweet became one of the most celebrated examples of real-time marketing in modern advertising history.

But beyond the applause lies a deeper martial lesson: tactical adaptability rooted in disciplined readiness.

1. **The Moment of Darkness**

   In sparring, opportunity rarely announces itself.

   It appears briefly — a slight opening, a misstep, a shift in balance.

   The Super Bowl blackout was such a moment.

   For most brands, it was an inconvenience.

   For Oreo, it was terrain.

   The team had prepared a war room for real-time social engagement. Designers, copywriters, and decision-makers were co-located, empowered to act without bureaucratic delay.

When the lights went out, they did not scramble.

They flowed.

2. **"Be Water": Fluid Response**

   The philosophy famously articulated by Bruce Lee — "Be like water" — captures the essence of Oreo's response.

   Water does not resist the container.

   It adapts to it.

   The blackout altered the arena. Oreo altered its messaging instantly.

   No elaborate campaign.

   No production delay.

   No overthinking.

   A simple visual.

   A timely line.

   Fluidity requires preparation.

   Spontaneity is often rehearsed readiness.

3. **Tactical Simplicity**

   The brilliance of "Dunk in the Dark" was not complexity. It was precision.

   The message:

   Was on-brand (dunking is central to Oreo identity)

   - Required no explanation
   - Used humor lightly
   - Felt culturally embedded

   In martial terms, it was a clean counterstrike.

   No flourish.

   No forced wit.

   Just relevance.

4. **Discipline behind Speed**

   Many brands misinterpret real-time marketing as improvisation.

   In truth, Oreo's success was built on structure:

   - Pre-approved brand guidelines

- Empowered decision-making authority
- Cross-functional coordination
- Clear tone discipline

Without internal discipline, speed becomes chaos.

Oreo's team had trained for the unexpected. The blackout merely activated muscle memory.

In the dojo, drills prepare for unplanned moments.

5. **The Power of Cultural Listening**

A martial artist reads the opponent.

A modern brand reads the culture.

The Super Bowl is not just a sporting event — it is a cultural spectacle. Oreo understood that social media conversation during the event was as important as the television broadcast.

By entering the live conversation organically, Oreo demonstrated cultural fluency.

It did not interrupt the moment.

It became part of it.

This is the essence of contextual awareness.

6. **Real-Time Marketing: Opportunity and Risk**

The success of "Dunk in the Dark" sparked a wave of brands seeking to engage in real time.

Many failed.

Why?

Because tactical adaptability without brand alignment feels opportunistic.

Oreo succeeded because:

- The message was true to the brand
- The tone matched its playful identity
- The timing felt natural

In martial arts, reacting without center leads to imbalance.

Real-time marketing must be anchored in identity.

7. **Fluidity as Competitive Edge**

   At a time when Super Bowl advertising slots cost millions, Oreo's most memorable moment cost virtually nothing beyond preparation.

   Fluidity outperformed budget.

   This is a critical strategic lesson:

   Resources matter.

   Responsiveness matters more.

   In saturated media environments, the brand that adapts in real time can capture disproportionate attention.

8. **Lessons for Marketers**

   From Oreo's "Dunk in the Dark," marketers can extract several dojo principles:

   1. *Prepare for the Unexpected*: Readiness enables agility.
   2. *Align Speed with Identity*: Fast responses must still feel authentic.
   3. *Keep it Simple*: Clarity wins over clever complexity.
   4. *Empower Decision-Makers*: Bureaucracy slows the strike.
   5. *Enter the Cultural Flow*: Relevance arises from listening, not forcing.

9. **The Discipline of Letting Go**

   Fluidity also means knowing when not to strike.

   After the viral success, Oreo did not overextend or over-exploit the moment. It allowed the impact to settle.

   In martial practice, restraint is as important as action.

   Not every opening demands engagement.

Closing Reflection

The "Dunk in the Dark" moment was not accidental brilliance.

It was disciplined adaptability.

It showed that when preparation meets opportunity, even a cookie can embody martial philosophy.

In the marketplace, darkness will come — disruptions, unexpected shifts, cultural interruptions.

The brand that flows with the moment, without losing its center, does not merely react.

It responds.

And in responding with clarity and timing, it turns interruption into mastery.

Case Study #8. Patagonia: Purpose-Driven Authenticity — The Harmony of Commerce and Conscience

In martial arts, the highest mastery is not domination.

It is alignment.

Alignment of technique with philosophy.

Alignment of strength with restraint.

Alignment of action with values.

Few brands embody this principle of alignment more completely than Patagonia.

In a world where purpose is often performed as marketing theater, Patagonia has practiced it as a discipline.

And discipline, over time, becomes identity.

1. **The Stance: Environmental Stewardship as Foundation**

   Founded by Yvon Chouinard, Patagonia was built on a simple conviction:

   Businesses should not merely extract value from nature.

   It should protect it.

   From its early days producing climbing equipment to its evolution into a global outdoor apparel brand, Patagonia's philosophy has remained clear: commerce and environmental responsibility must coexist.

   This is not a campaign theme.

   It is the stance.

   In martial arts, the stance determines every subsequent movement.

2. **"Don't Buy this Jacket": The Counterintuitive Strike**

   In 2011, Patagonia ran a Black Friday advertisement with a striking headline:

   "Don't Buy This Jacket."

The ad urged consumers to consider the environmental cost of their purchases before making a purchase.

At first glance, it appeared commercially irrational.

Why would a company discourage buying its own product?

From a martial perspective, this was a disciplined counterstrike.

Instead of competing through volume and discounting, Patagonia reframed the arena: sustainability over impulse.

The message was clear:

Buy less.

Choose well.

Make it last.

This move strengthened trust rather than weakened sales.

Authenticity, when genuine, creates loyalty deeper than transaction.

3. Harmony, Not Opposition

In traditional martial philosophy, strength and compassion are not opposites.

They are complements.

Patagonia demonstrates that profit and purpose need not be adversaries.

The company has:

- Donated 1% of sales to environmental causes
- Encouraged product repair through its "Worn Wear" program
- Advocated publicly for climate action
- Structured its ownership to ensure long-term environmental commitment

In 2022, Yvon Chouinard transferred ownership of Patagonia to a trust and nonprofit entity to ensure that profits would support environmental protection.

This was not branding.

It was structural alignment.

In dojo terms, philosophy became architecture.

4. Authenticity as Consistency Over Time

Purpose-driven marketing is often vulnerable to skepticism.

Consumers increasingly question whether values are genuine or opportunistic.

Patagonia's advantage lies in duration.

For decades, its messaging, policies, and corporate behavior have aligned.

Consistency builds credibility.

In martial arts, reputation is earned through repeated demonstration, not a single exhibition.

5. **Restraint in Growth**

   Many companies pursue expansion relentlessly.

   Patagonia has occasionally limited growth to maintain quality and environmental standards.

   This restraint mirrors a martial principle:

   Just because you can strike does not mean you should.

   Restraint signals control.

   Control signals mastery.

6. **The Risk of Moral Positioning**

   Purpose-driven brands face heightened scrutiny.

   Any inconsistency is magnified.

   Patagonia has navigated criticism about its supply chains and material sourcing—a reminder that ethical positioning requires continuous vigilance.

   Authenticity is not a fixed achievement.

   It is an ongoing practice.

   In martial arts, mastery is never declared permanent. It must be renewed daily.

7. **Emotional Resonance through Integrity**

   Patagonia's customers often describe emotional loyalty that transcends product attributes.

   Why?

   Because alignment creates resonance.

   When consumers perceive harmony between message and behavior, trust deepens.

Trust reduces price sensitivity.

Trust increases advocacy.

Trust sustains resilience.

Commerce strengthened by conscience becomes durable.

8. **Lessons for Marketers**

   From Patagonia's example, marketers can extract powerful dojo principles:

   1. *Anchor Strategy in Philosophy*: Purpose must guide decision-making, not decorate it.
   2. *Align Structure With Values*: Authenticity requires operational integrity.
   3. *Embrace Counterintuitive Courage*: Sometimes discouraging consumption strengthens brand loyalty.
   4. *Consistency Builds Moral Authority*: Purpose must endure beyond campaigns.
   5. *Practice Ongoing Accountability*: Ethical positioning demands vigilance.

9. **Harmony as Competitive Advantage**

   In competitive markets, brands often escalate through aggression — louder messaging, deeper discounts, broader expansion.

   Patagonia chose harmony.

   Harmony between profit and planet.

   Between product and principle.

   Between commerce and conscience.

   This harmony became differentiation.

   While others compete for attention, Patagonia competes for alignment.

Closing Reflection

In martial arts, the ultimate goal is not victory over others.

It is integration within oneself.

Patagonia demonstrates that brands can pursue growth without abandoning values — that commercial success and ethical responsibility can coexist when disciplined by philosophy.

The harmony of commerce and conscience is not weakness.

It is strength refined by restraint.

And in that harmony, a brand does not merely sell.

It stands.

Case Study #9. Peloton: Community-Based Growth — The Martial Model of Shared Struggle and Discipline

In martial arts, mastery is individual.

But it is never solitary.

The lone practitioner in a dojo still trains within a community. The shared rhythm of breath, the synchronized repetition of drills, the collective silence before sparring — these elements create momentum beyond personal effort.

Peloton understood this truth and built a brand not merely around equipment, but around shared discipline.

Its rise illustrates a powerful marketing principle: community is not an accessory to growth. It is a multiplier.

1. The Dojo at Home

When Peloton launched, the home fitness category was largely transactional:

- Buy equipment.
- Use it alone.
- Hope for consistency.

Peloton reframed the experience.

Instead of selling a stationary bike, it sold access to a live, instructor-led, digitally connected community.

Users could see:

- Leaderboards
- Class participation
- Real-time metrics
- Instructor shout-outs

In martial terms, Peloton transported the dojo into the home.

The practitioner was physically alone but socially connected.

This shift changed the emotional equation of exercise.

2. **Shared Struggle as Bonding**

   In martial arts, shared hardship builds cohesion.

   The sweat of synchronized drills.

   The exhaustion of repeated rounds.

   The quiet acknowledgment between sparring partners.

   Peloton replicated this through:

   - Live class energy
   - Instructor motivation
   - Milestone celebrations
   - Hashtag-based micro-communities

   Members identified not merely as customers, but as participants in a shared discipline.

   The brand did not promise ease.

   It promised effort — together.

   Shared struggle became emotional glue.

3. **Discipline through Ritual**

   One of Peloton's strengths lies in ritualization.

   - Scheduled live classes
   - Recurring instructors
   - Progress tracking
   - Achievement badges

   Ritual reinforces commitment.

   In martial arts, belts mark progression. Drills structure repetition. The environment shapes habit.

   Peloton introduced digital equivalents:

   - Metrics dashboards
   - Streaks
   - Performance graphs

   These elements transformed exercise into a structured progression.

   Marketing here was not persuasion.

   It was the facilitation of discipline.

4. **Instructor as Sensei**

   Peloton instructors function as modern senseis.

   They are not merely trainers.

   They are motivators, storytellers, culture carriers.

   Their personalities — intense, empathetic, humorous — become extensions of the brand.

   In the dojo, the teacher shapes the practitioner's mindset.

   Peloton's instructors shape identity:

   "You showed up."

   "You didn't quit."

   "You earned this."

   These affirmations cultivate belonging.

   Belonging sustains engagement.

5. **Network Effects as Collective Momentum**

   Community-based growth creates self-reinforcing dynamics.

   As membership increased, energy intensified.

   As energy intensified, brand advocacy expanded.

   Users shared milestones on social media.

   Friends joined.

   Communities formed around shared hashtags.

   This resembles dojo expansion: as more practitioners join, the environment becomes richer, attracting more entrants.

   Momentum builds organically.

6. **The Risk of Overextension**

   Like any martial practitioner who expands too quickly, Peloton encountered challenges.

   Rapid growth during the COVID-19 pandemic created operational strain. Post-pandemic demand shifts exposed overexpansion in manufacturing and inventory.

   The lesson here is balance.

   Shared struggle builds strength.

   Overreach creates vulnerability.

Discipline must extend to operational strategy as well as brand community.

7. **Identity beyond Equipment**

   Peloton's most significant strategic move was redefining its category.

   It is not a bike company.

   It is a connected fitness community.

   This shift mirrors martial philosophy: the weapon is secondary. The practitioner is primary.

   The hardware enables practice.

   The community sustains commitment.

8. **Lessons for Marketers**

   From Peloton's journey, several dojo principles emerge:

   1. *Community Drives Retention*: Belonging strengthens loyalty more than features.
   2. *Ritual Builds Discipline*: Structured routines increase engagement.
   3. *Shared Struggle Creates Bond*: Effort binds participants emotionally.
   4. *Empower Leaders*: Instructors (or brand ambassadors) embody culture.
   5. *Balance Growth with Control*: Momentum must be matched by operational discipline.

9. **Marketing as Collective Practice**

   Peloton demonstrates that marketing need not always emphasize differentiation through product features.

   It can emphasize participation.

   In martial arts, mastery is cultivated through collective repetition.

   In marketing, brand mastery can emerge through shared experience.

   Peloton's genius was recognizing that in an increasingly isolated digital world, a structured community could become a premium offering.

Closing Reflection

In the dojo, progress is visible not only in belts but in the community's energy.

Peloton built a brand where every ride felt like sparring alongside thousands — alone, yet together.

The martial lesson is clear:

Discipline deepens when shared.

Struggle strengthens when communal.

Growth accelerates when belonging is real.

A brand that builds community does not merely acquire customers.

It cultivates practitioners.

And practitioners return again and again.

Case Study #10. Spotify "Wrapped": Personalization as Fluid Storytelling — Adaptability Through Data Empathy

In martial arts, awareness precedes action.

The master reads subtle shifts — breath, stance, intention — and responds not mechanically, but intuitively.

Spotify demonstrates a similar principle through its annual "Wrapped" campaign.

What began as a simple year-end listening summary evolved into a global cultural ritual — a moment when millions of users share their musical identities with pride.

Wrapped is not merely data visualization.

It is fluid storytelling shaped by empathy.

1. **From Metrics to Meaning**

   Streaming platforms collect enormous amounts of behavioral data:

   - Songs played
   - Genres explored
   - Minutes streamed
   - Artists revisited

   Data alone is sterile.

   Wrapped transformed metrics into a narrative.

   Instead of saying, "You listened to 1,250 minutes of pop," Spotify reframed it as:

   "You were in the top 1% of fans."

   "You had a 'Main Character 'year."

   "You explored five new genres."

   This is storytelling through personalization.

   In martial terms, it is not enough to know the opponent's movements. One must interpret intention.

   Spotify interpreted user behavior and reflected it back as identity.

2. **Fluidity through Adaptation**

   Each year, Wrapped evolves.

   New design styles.

   New cultural references.

   New shareable formats.

   The campaign does not remain fixed.

   It adapts to:

   - Meme culture
   - Platform trends
   - Visual design shifts
   - Social sharing habits

   Fluidity here is intentional.

   Like water, Wrapped flows into the containers of contemporary digital culture.

   But its essence remains stable:

   "You are seen."

3. **Data Empathy: Reading the Practitioner**

   In the dojo, a skilled teacher adjusts instruction based on the student's strengths and weaknesses.

   Spotify applies similar empathy through data.

   It does not treat users as a monolith.

   It recognizes individual taste patterns and celebrates them.

   This celebration builds emotional connection.

   The message is subtle but powerful:

   Your choices matter.

   Your taste is unique.

   Your year had a soundtrack.

   This is not personalization as algorithmic efficiency.

   It is personalization as recognition.

4. **Ritual as Cultural Kata**

   Wrapped is anticipated.

Users expect it each December.

This annual cadence creates ritual.

In martial arts, rituals structure growth — grading ceremonies, seasonal tournaments, and annual gatherings.

Spotify's ritual transforms data into a communal event.

Millions share their Wrapped summaries simultaneously.

Individual stories converge into a collective culture.

5. **Shareability as Social Sparring**

   Wrapped is inherently social.

   Its vertical slides, bold typography, and playful categories are designed for sharing.

   When users post their Wrapped results, they engage in a kind of cultural sparring:

   - Comparing tastes
   - Celebrating overlaps
   - Discovering differences

   The campaign extends beyond private reflection into public identity.

   This multiplies reach organically.

   Marketing becomes participatory.

6. **Adaptability Under Pressure**

   Digital environments shift quickly.

   Platform algorithms change. Attention spans shorten.

   Spotify maintains relevance by adjusting design language and cultural references each year.

   Yet the core principle remains:

   Data as storytelling.

   Storytelling as identity affirmation.

   Fluidity anchored in purpose.

7. **The Risk of Over-Personalization**

   Personalization requires trust.

   Users must feel that data is used to celebrate, not exploit.

Spotify navigates this by maintaining a playful tone and a voluntary sharing model.

The data presented feels empowering rather than invasive.

Empathy tempers analytics.

8. **Lessons for Marketers**

   From Spotify Wrapped, marketers can extract several dojo principles:

   1. *Transform Data into Narrative*: Numbers gain power when shaped into a story.
   2. *Build Ritual into Campaigns*: Consistency creates anticipation.
   3. *Adapt Aesthetics without Losing Core*: Fluid form, stable philosophy.
   4. *Celebrate the Individual*: Recognition builds loyalty.
   5. *Design for Sharing*: Participation amplifies impact.

9. **Fluid Storytelling as Strategic Advantage**

   Wrapped demonstrates that personalization can be more than recommendation engines.

   It can be cultural theater.

   Each year, Spotify turns introspection into celebration.

   The campaign costs less than major advertising blitzes yet generates massive organic engagement.

   Why?

   Because it flows naturally from user behavior.

   It feels earned.

Closing Reflection

In martial arts, the highest awareness is not rigid calculation.

It is responsive empathy.

Spotify's Wrapped campaign shows that data, when shaped by empathy, becomes narrative fluidity.

The brand listens.

Interprets.

Reflects.

And in that reflection, users see themselves.

A brand that makes people feel seen does not merely provide a service.

It builds connection.

And connection, practiced annually with discipline and creativity, becomes ritual.

Case Study #11. Toyota: Kaizen Philosophy in Brand and Process — Martial Discipline in Corporate Culture

In martial arts, mastery is not achieved through dramatic breakthroughs.

It is achieved through daily refinement.

A slight correction in stance.

A subtle adjustment in grip.

A repeated drill performed with greater awareness than the day before.

This philosophy of incremental improvement is embedded at the core of Toyota — a company whose competitive strength has long rested not on theatrical marketing, but on disciplined process.

The Japanese principle of Kaizen — continuous improvement — mirrors the martial path toward mastery.

And Toyota institutionalized it.

1. **Kaizen: Improvement as Ritual**

   Kaizen does not promise revolution.

   It promises repetition with reflection.

   From factory floors to executive meetings, Toyota cultivated a culture where every employee is encouraged to identify inefficiencies and propose improvements.

   This is not merely an operational policy.

   It is philosophical discipline.

   In the dojo, every practitioner, regardless of belt rank, participates in refining technique.

   Toyota applied this democratized discipline to manufacturing.

2. **The Toyota Production System: Structured Kata**

   Toyota's operational excellence became globally studied through the Toyota Production System (TPS).

   Its pillars include:

   - Just-in-Time production

- Jidoka (automation with human oversight)
- Waste elimination
- Respect for people

These are not isolated techniques. They form a system — like a carefully structured martial kata.

Each step reinforces the next.

Each correction prevents error accumulation.

In martial arts, sloppy repetition compounds weakness. In manufacturing, inefficiency compounds cost.

Toyota's discipline reduced variability and enhanced reliability.

3. **Brand as Reflection of Process**

Marketing often exists separately from operations.

At Toyota, brand perception emerged from process consistency.

The company became associated with:

- Reliability
- Efficiency
- Longevity
- Practical innovation

These attributes were not invented in advertising.

They were earned in production.

This alignment reflects a martial truth: External strength reflects internal training.

When corporate culture embodies discipline, brand messaging requires less embellishment.

4. **Resilience through Discipline**

The true test of discipline is not during smooth operation, but during disruption.

In 2009–2010, Toyota faced a major recall crisis related to vehicle safety concerns.

The crisis threatened its reputation for reliability.

The company's response demonstrated martial composure:

- Public acknowledgment
- Process review
- Reinforcement of quality controls

- Long-term corrective measures

Recovery was not immediate.

But a disciplined response restored trust over time.

In martial arts, recovery from imbalance defines mastery.

5. **Incremental Innovation vs. Flashy Reinvention**

   Toyota has historically favored incremental improvement over dramatic transformation.

   While competitors pursued aggressive styling or radical repositioning, Toyota refined core engineering.

   This is not conservatism.

   It is a structured progression.

   In martial arts training, advancing from one belt to the next involves gradual mastery, not sudden leaps.

   Incremental innovation builds durable strength.

6. **Expansion with Philosophy Intact**

   Toyota's global expansion maintained key elements of its philosophy while adapting to local markets.

   Factories abroad adopted Kaizen principles. Employees worldwide were trained in structured improvement practices.

   Fluid expansion, anchored in stable philosophy.

   This balance mirrors that of advanced martial practitioners, who adapt to varied terrains while maintaining core technique.

7. **The Discipline of Long-Term Thinking**

   Kaizen requires patience.

   Short-term financial gains may tempt shortcuts in cost-cutting.

   But disciplined cultures prioritize sustainable excellence.

   Toyota's long-term orientation contrasts with the quarterly performance-driven volatility seen elsewhere.

   Martial mastery, too, rejects shortcuts.

   Enduring skill cannot be rushed.

8. **Lessons for Marketers**

   From Toyota's disciplined philosophy, marketers can extract powerful dojo insights:

   1. *Build Brand from Process*: An authentic reputation grows from operational integrity.

2. *Institutionalize Improvement:* Continuous refinement compounds competitive advantage.
3. *Empower the Frontline*: Respect for people strengthens systems.
4. *Respond to Crisis with Composure*: Discipline under pressure restores trust.
5. *Favor Long-Term Mastery Over Short-Term Hype*: Sustained credibility outperforms spectacle.

9. Harmony between Form and Function

Toyota's vehicles may not always be the flashiest, but they are often among the most dependable.

This harmony between function and form mirrors martial arts philosophy:

True strength does not need excessive display.

The company's commitment to hybrid technology, including leadership in fuel-efficient vehicles, further reflects alignment between innovation and responsibility.

Steady, disciplined, purposeful.

Closing Reflection

In martial arts, the highest mastery is often invisible.

It resides in the quiet repetition of fundamentals.

Toyota demonstrates that corporate excellence can mirror dojo discipline — structured, patient, humble, and continuously improving.

The brand does not shout.

It practices.

And in that disciplined practice, reliability becomes reputation.

Reputation becomes trust.

Trust becomes an enduring strength.

Case Study #12. UFC and Conor McGregor: The Fighter as Brand — Identity-Based Storytelling and Persona Mastery

In martial arts, skill wins bouts.

But identity wins arenas.

Technique earns respect.

Persona commands attention.

Few modern figures illustrate this fusion of combat and branding more vividly than the Ultimate Fighting Championship and its most polarizing star, Conor McGregor.

Together, they transformed the fighter from competitor to cultural brand.

1. **The Evolution of the Fighter**

   Early mixed martial arts events emphasized technique over narrative.

   Fighters were presented as specialists — wrestlers, strikers, jiu-jitsu practitioners — defined by style more than personality.

   As the UFC matured into a global sports entertainment platform, it recognized a deeper truth:

   Fights sell.

   But stories scale.

   The organization began spotlighting backstories, rivalries, and personal journeys. The octagon became a stage not only for physical confrontation, but for identity performance.

   In martial terms, this was a shift from pure sparring to theatrical combat, where persona amplifies technique.

2. **Conor McGregor: Persona as Weapon**

   Conor McGregor did not merely fight.

   He narrated his fights before they happened.

   With sharp wit, bold predictions, and flamboyant self-assurance, he crafted an unmistakable persona:

- The brash challenger
- The precision striker
- The self-proclaimed "Notorious."

He declared outcomes in advance. He framed opponents as chapters in his own story of ascension.

This was psychological sparring long before physical engagement.

In the dojo, confidence destabilizes the opponent.

In marketing, confidence commands attention.

3. **Identity-Based Storytelling**

McGregor's narrative rested on powerful themes:

- The underdog rising from Dublin
- The immigrant's hunger
- The audacious believer
- The disciplined striker who visualizes victory

These themes resonated beyond MMA audiences.

Fans did not merely watch fights.

They invested in identity.

This is identity-based storytelling at its peak.

The fighter became a symbol of defiance, ambition, and swagger.

4. **The UFC's Strategic Amplification**

The UFC understood the commercial potential of personality.

By amplifying press conferences, embedding dramatic build-ups, and distributing behind-the-scenes content, the organization expanded the narrative field.

It became less about a single bout and more about episodic storytelling.

In martial arts terms, this is expanding the arena.

Every interview, stare-down, and social media post became part of the fight.

The persona generated anticipation.

Anticipation generated pay-per-view sales.

5. **Persona Mastery: Discipline behind Bravado**

   It is easy to mistake McGregor's persona for improvisation.

   But persona mastery requires discipline.

   - Consistent tone
   - Repeated narrative themes
   - Controlled unpredictability
   - Calculated risk-taking

   The character was not random.

   It was strategically reinforced.

   In martial training, repeated forms build identity.

   In branding, repeated messaging builds recognition.

6. **Risk and Volatility**

   Identity-based branding carries risk.

   Persona magnifies both success and failure.

   Losses in the octagon affected McGregor's aura. Public controversies complicated brand perception.

   Here lies the martial lesson:

   When the persona becomes larger than the practice, an imbalance emerges.

   Sustained mastery requires alignment between narrative and performance.

7. **From Athlete to Enterprise**

   McGregor extended his brand beyond fighting:

   - Whiskey ventures
   - Apparel
   - Media appearances

   This transition reflects a shift from athlete identity to entrepreneurial identity.

   The fighter became a brand platform.

   The UFC benefited from this amplification, reinforcing its image as a theater of bold personalities rather than anonymous competitors.

8. Lessons for Marketers

From UFC and McGregor's rise, marketers can extract powerful dojo principles:

1. *Identity Drives Engagement*: People connect more deeply with personas than with products.
2. *Narrative Precedes Action*: Anticipation increases perceived significance.
3. *Consistency Shapes Recognition*: A repeated persona strengthens brand recall.
4. *Amplify Beyond the Core Product*: Content ecosystems expand influence.
5. *Balance Persona with Performance*: Sustained credibility requires alignment.

9. The Martial Mirror

In traditional martial arts, humility is emphasized.

In modern combat sports, personality is amplified.

The tension between discipline and bravado creates spectacle.

The UFC harnessed this tension commercially.

McGregor embodied it culturally.

Together, they illustrate that in the modern marketplace, identity can function as strategic leverage — but only when backed by authentic skill.

Closing Reflection

In the dojo, mastery begins with technique.

In the arena, mastery includes presence.

The UFC and Conor McGregor demonstrate that storytelling and persona can transform a fighter into a brand — and a brand into cultural currency.

But the martial lesson endures:

A persona may attract the crowd.

Skill sustains the legacy.

And true mastery lies in balancing both.

Appendix A

Quotes from Martial Artists and Marketing Visionaries

In both martial arts and marketing, the masters distill complexity into clarity. Their wisdom is often delivered in aphorisms — brief, sharp, and transformative. The following collection bridges the dojo and the boardroom, showing how the pursuit of mastery, integrity, and awareness unites them across centuries and disciplines.

1. **On Mastery and Practice**

   "I fear not the man who has practiced 10,000 kicks once, but I fear the man who has practiced one kick 10,000 times."

   — Bruce Lee

   Every marketer who has refined a single campaign insight until it resonates knows this truth. Repetition breeds instinct, and instinct breeds mastery.

   "We are what we repeatedly do. Excellence, then, is not an act, but a habit."

   — Aristotle

   Brand consistency, like kata in martial arts, transforms repetition into identity. Excellence becomes muscle memory.

   "The successful warrior is the average man, with laser-like focus."

   — Bruce Lee

   Focus, not frenzy, builds dominance. Every enduring brand — from Apple to Nike — won through disciplined simplicity, not scattered energy.

2. **On Adaptability and Change**

   "Be water, my friend."

   — Bruce Lee

Fluidity is the essence of survival — in combat and commerce. The brand that clings to form perishes; the one that flows endures.

"You must be shapeless, formless, like water. When you pour water in a cup, it becomes the cup."

— Bruce Lee

This is design thinking before its time — the art of dissolving boundaries between company and customer, between message and medium.

"In the midst of chaos, there is also opportunity."

— Sun Tzu, The Art of War

Every market disruption is a hidden invitation. The martial artist sees in unpredictability the perfect moment for transformation; the marketer sees a shift in consumer behavior — and responds with agility, not panic.

3. **On Ethics, Purpose, and the Inner Path**

"The ultimate aim of martial arts is not having to use them."

— Miyamoto Musashi

The truest marketers, too, reach a point where persuasion gives way to trust — where the product's integrity sells itself.

"Perception precedes reality."

— Andy Warhol

The artist and the marketer share this secret: meaning is shaped by perception, not production. Authenticity is not what you say, but how consistently you live it.

"People don't buy what you do; they buy why you do it."

— Simon Sinek

Purpose is the invisible hand behind both powerful art and enduring enterprise.

"To win one hundred victories in one hundred battles is not the highest skill. To subdue the enemy without fighting is the highest skill."

— Sun Tzu

The marketer's highest art, like the martial artist's, is harmony — achieving persuasion without pressure, influence without intrusion.

4. **On Learning and Growth**

"There are no limits — only plateaus. And you must not stay there; you must go beyond them."

— Bruce Lee

Both arts teach that the moment you stop learning, you start losing. Mastery demands constant reinvention.

"Failure is simply the opportunity to begin again, this time more intelligently."

— Henry Ford

A failed campaign, like a failed match, is a teacher. Both invite humility — and the promise of refinement.

"If you always do what you've always done, you'll always get what you've always got."

— Tony Robbins

Adaptation is the lifeblood of evolution — in technique and in storytelling alike.

"Mastery is not a function of genius or talent. It is a function of time and intense focus applied to a particular field of knowledge."

— Robert Greene, Mastery

The dojo and the data lab operate by the same law: mastery is earned, not granted.

Appendix B

Sample Campaign Templates Inspired by Martial Arts Principles

These templates are not formulas but frameworks — modern marketing katas inspired by the timeless logic of martial disciplines. Each one distills a core martial concept into an actionable campaign model.

1. **The "Be Like Water" Campaign Framework**

   Core Principle: Adaptability to context

   Marketing Translation: Dynamic personalization based on consumer mood and moment

   Application Steps:

   1. Listen — Analyze sentiment in real-time (social media, forums, feedback loops).
   2. Flow — Adapt tone, imagery, or timing dynamically (content calibrated by data).
   3. Reflect — Measure emotional resonance, not just engagement.
   4. Refine — Adjust the message continuously, like a fighter reading their opponent.

   Example: Spotify's "Wrapped" campaign — fluidly personalized, turning audience behavior into celebration.

2. **The "White Belt to Black Belt" Learning Journey**

   Core Principle: Continuous improvement through structured mastery

   Marketing Translation: Build customer loyalty through progressive engagement

Application Steps:

1. Initiation (White Belt): Awareness campaigns introducing the brand philosophy.
2. Commitment (Blue Belt): Gamified challenges or educational content deepening understanding.
3. Fluency (Brown Belt): Community participation, user-generated storytelling.
4. Mastery (Black Belt): Advocacy — Customers Become Ambassadors.

Example: Nike Run Club and Duolingo's gamified mastery paths — where progress itself becomes the product.

3. **The "Zen Strike" Minimalist Messaging Model**

Core Principle: Simplicity, focus, precision

Marketing Translation: Deliver one message, perfectly timed

Application Steps:

1. Clarity: Strip away every secondary message — focus on one core idea.
2. Timing: Release with cultural awareness — when the audience is most receptive.
3. Impact: Use silence and space (visual or narrative) to amplify focus.
4. Reflection: Allow time for resonance before the next communication.

Example: Apple's products reveal minimalist storytelling, maximal anticipation.

4. **The "Dojo of the Brand" Internal Culture Canvas**

Core Principle: Mastery through mindset

Marketing Translation: Align teams through shared rituals and values

Implementation Framework:

- Code of Honor: Define core brand ethics (truth, respect, consistency).
- Daily Practice: Embed rituals — stand-ups, reflections, shared metrics.

- Mentorship: Senior marketers act as senseis, guiding juniors through apprenticeship.
- Feedback Sparring: Encourage peer-to-peer reviews framed as learning opportunities rather than critiques.

Example: Pixar's "Braintrust" sessions — structured, honest, respectful feedback that refines ideas without ego.

5. **The "Art of Anticipation" Strategic Playbook**

Core Principle: Read the opponent, not just the moment

Marketing Translation: Predict market shifts before they happen

Application Steps:

1. Observe: Study weak signals — early trends, consumer anxiety, cultural whispers.
2. Anticipate: Map possible outcomes, like a fighter visualizing an opponent's counter.
3. Position: Prepare adaptable campaigns — ready to pivot on timing or tone.
4. Strike: Execute precisely when attention and need align.

Example: Netflix's early pivot to streaming, or Oreo's "You can still dunk in the dark" — moments where perception beat preparation.

6. **The "Master and Apprentice" Mentorship Framework**

Core Principle: Skill transfer through relationship

Marketing Translation: Institutionalize knowledge-sharing and legacy-building

Implementation Steps:

1. Pairing: Match senior strategists with emerging talent across projects.
2. Observation: Apprentices shadow live campaigns before leading smaller ones.
3. Feedback Loop: Regular one-on-one reflections — learning codified into best practices.
4. Lineage Building: Celebrate each generation's contribution to the craft.

Example: Ogilvy's mentorship culture — a lineage of excellence where creative DNA is consciously passed down.

7. **The "Flow State" Team Framework**

   Core Principle: Presence, immersion, synchronization

   Marketing Translation: Design work environments that cultivate collective flow

   Application Steps:

   1. Eliminate Noise: Remove non-essential meetings and notifications during creative cycles.
   2. Shared Rhythm: Work in timed "sprints" or "rounds," balancing effort and rest.
   3. Instant Feedback: Encourage live testing and quick iteration.
   4. Celebrate Immersion: Recognize focus as much as output.

   Example: IDEO's design sessions — cross-disciplinary, time-boxed, and immersive, mirroring the harmony of a martial sparring rhythm.

8. **The "Belt of Integrity" Ethical Marketing Charter**

   Core Principle: Honor and accountability

   Marketing Translation: Codify ethics as a competitive advantage

   Elements:

   - Transparency: Full disclosure in claims and partnerships.
   - Respect: Consent and Dignity in Data Use.
   - Courage: Standing by values in crises, even at cost.
   - Self-Reflection: Annual ethical audit — the brand equivalent of a belt test.

   Example: Patagonia's "Don't Buy This Jacket" — a counterintuitive campaign that elevated trust over sales.

C. Closing Reflection: The Dojo of Modern Marketing

The dojo and the brand both serve the same purpose: they are spaces of transformation. One trains the body; the other, the mind of the market. But the path through both is identical — discipline, empathy, adaptability, and continuous refinement.

When marketers practice their art like martial artists — with humility before complexity and respect before competition — marketing transcends manipulation. It becomes movement.

As Bruce Lee once said,

"Knowing is not enough; we must apply. Willing is not enough; we must do."

The future of marketing belongs not to the loudest, but to the most conscious. The master marketer, like the master martial artist, knows that victory is never final — only practice is.

Appendix C

Core Concepts and Philosophies

Adaptability: Principle of flexibility in both combat and marketing; "Be Like Water" philosophy; case study: Netflix and Spotify.

Antifragility: Concept by Nassim Nicholas Taleb; resilience through stress; parallels between market crises and martial recovery.

Awareness: Zanshin in martial arts; market perception, audience listening, and mindfulness as strategic tools.

Balance: Mental, emotional, and ethical equilibrium in branding and self-mastery.

Be Like Water (Philosophy): Bruce Lee's concept of formlessness, applied to adaptability, enhances campaign flexibility and creativity.

Bushidō (Way of the Warrior): Ethical code of samurai: parallels in marketing ethics and purpose-driven leadership.

Character and Integrity: Foundational values in both arts: reflections on ethical persuasion and authentic branding.

Competition: Rivalries as mirrors; martial contests compared with brand positioning battles.

Conscious Marketing: An ethical and mindful approach, combining strategy, empathy, and responsibility.

Discipline: Repetition as mastery; process and precision over spontaneity; grit as the unseen differentiator.

Dojo Mindset: A continuous learning environment; the marketer's dojo as a metaphor for lifelong growth.

Ethics in Marketing: Transparency, honesty, and consumer respect as moral equivalents of martial codes.

Flow State: Csikszentmihalyi's theory of immersion: team synchronization in creative work.

Growth Mindset: Carol Dweck's principle applied to marketers 'learning paths and adaptability.

Humility: Beginner's mind (shoshin) and its role in reinvention and creative openness.

Kaizen (Continuous Improvement): From martial training to Toyota's philosophy, application to campaign refinement.

Kata (Form and Ritual): Structured repetition in martial practice; marketing equivalents in process and consistency.

Mastery: Repetition and refinement; deliberate practice as the cornerstone of excellence.

Mindfulness: Awareness in action: the role of presence in decision-making and design.

Purpose-Driven Marketing: Connection between brand values and audience identity; parallels to Do.

Resilience: Antifragility and adaptability under market pressure; learning from defeat.

Respect (Rei): Foundation of both arts; acknowledgment of mentors, competitors, and consumers.

Strategy and Timing: Tactical and temporal intelligence: parallels between Sun Tzu's timing and marketing agility.

Zen and Stillness: The paradox of calm action, clarity in motion and patience in practice.

Appendix D

Martial Arts Schools, Philosophies, and Historical Figures

Aikido: Non-aggressive redirection; applied to conflict-free persuasion and crisis management.

Brazilian Jiu-Jitsu (BJJ): Grassroots growth model; community marketing and loyalty-building.

Bruce Lee: Adaptability, mastery, formlessness; "Be Water" and cross-disciplinary inspiration.

Funakoshi, Gichin: Philosophy of humility and perseverance; parallels to long-term brand ethics.

Gracie Family: BJJ pioneers, storytelling, and authenticity as community-building tools.

Jeet Kune Do: "Using no way as way"; parallel to integrated, cross-platform marketing.

Jigoro Kano (Judo): "Gentle way" philosophy; efficiency, leverage, and education as brand metaphors.

Karate: Discipline, respect, ritual; structure as a foundation of creativity.

Miyamoto Musashi: Strategy of awareness and simplicity: The Book of Five Rings' influence on marketing minimalism.

Sun Tzu: Strategic philosophy: anticipation, deception, and adaptability as marketing parallels.

Ueshiba, Morihei: Founder of Aikido; harmony and peace as higher goals of influence.

Zen Buddhism: Non-attachment, mindfulness, and balance as creative principles.

Appendix E

Marketing Frameworks and Models Referenced

4Ps of Marketing (E. Jerome McCarthy): Product, price, place, promotion; reinterpreted through the martial lens of balance.

Brand Equity: Trust as cumulative mastery; the "black belt" of marketing outcomes.

Consumer Journey Mapping: Awareness, consideration, engagement, loyalty, compared to the martial belt hierarchy.

Digital Transformation: From print to AI; parallels with martial evolution from rigid to fluid systems.

Ethical Branding Charter ("Belt of Integrity"): Framework for transparency, respect, and long-term reputation.

Flow Framework (Team Synchrony): Group performance model; inspiration from dojo rhythm and sparring balance.

Kata in Campaign Planning: Ritualized practice model for consistent creativity.

Mentorship Framework ("Master and Apprentice"): Knowledge transmission; lineage-building within marketing teams.

Omnichannel Strategy as MMA: Integration across platforms; blending specialization and synthesis.

Purpose and Storytelling: Narrative resonance through archetype and ethos; case study: Dove, Nike, Patagonia.

Resonance Marketing: Emotional frequency matching between the brand and the audience, derived from empathy training principles.

Strategic Playbook ("Art of Anticipation"): Early detection, timing, and adaptability modeled after martial reading of opponents.

Appendix F

Scholars, Theorists, and Thinkers Cited

Csikszentmihalyi, Mihaly: Flow theory, applied to marketing creativity and team synchronization.

Drucker, Peter: Marketing as understanding, not persuasion; business philosophy aligned with Do.

Duckworth, Angela: Grit and perseverance: the neuroscience of long-term effort.

Dweck, Carol: Growth mindset; continuous learning culture.

E. Jerome McCarthy: 4-P Marketing Framework

Ericsson, Anders: Deliberate practice model: foundation of mastery.

Kahneman, Daniel: Behavioral economics; System 1 and 2 thinking in consumer decision-making.

Kotler, Philip: Core marketing frameworks: bridge between strategy and service.

Sinek, Simon: Purpose-driven leadership and storytelling.

Taleb, Nassim Nicholas: Antifragility: strength through volatility.

Sun Tzu: Timeless guide on strategy and anticipation.

The overlap between marketing and martial arts is not metaphorical — it is mechanical, philosophical, and moral. Both are lifelong practices of awareness, precision, and empathy. The true index of mastery is not in how much one remembers, but in how one embodies what matters.

Glossary of Key Terms

A

Adaptability

The capacity to adjust tactics and mindset in response to changing circumstances. In martial arts, it's the ability to flow with an opponent's energy; in marketing, it's the agility to pivot strategies in dynamic markets. Embodied in Bruce Lee's dictum, "Be like water."

Aikido

A Japanese martial art founded by Morihei Ueshiba, emphasizing harmony and redirection of force rather than confrontation. Aikido principles mirror conflict-free negotiation, empathetic persuasion, and crisis management in marketing.

Antifragility

A concept from Nassim Nicholas Taleb describing systems that grow stronger through volatility and stress. In marketing, brands that learn from failure and evolve under pressure embody the concept of antifragility.

Archetype

A universally recognizable character or story pattern used in branding and storytelling (e.g., Hero, Sage, Rebel). Derived from Jungian psychology, archetypes help brands resonate emotionally and culturally.

Awareness (Zanshin)

A continuous, heightened state of focus. In martial arts, zanshin means remaining alert before, during, and after action. In marketing, it translates to constant awareness of consumer sentiment and competitive shifts.

B

Balance

The state of equilibrium between effort and ease, offense and defense. In branding, it's the equilibrium between creativity and data, speed and strategy, innovation and consistency.

Be Like Water

Bruce Lee's central philosophy advocates flexibility, fluidity, and responsiveness. A metaphor for brands that flow with consumer needs and technological change without losing identity.

Brand Equity

The cumulative value of a brand's reputation, recognition, and customer trust — the "black belt" of marketing achievement.

Bushidō

The ancient Japanese "Way of the Warrior" emphasizes honor, respect, discipline, and moral purpose. Its principles — courage, integrity, compassion — parallel modern ethical marketing.

C

Campaign Kata

A structured, repeatable process for planning and refining marketing campaigns. Adapted from kata in martial arts — choreographed routines practiced until instinctive.

Character

The ethical and emotional identity of both a martial artist and a brand. Integrity sustains both trust and mastery.

Competition (Randori)

In martial arts, free sparring hones awareness and adaptability. In marketing, competition serves as a form of feedback, refining both purpose and performance.

Consumer Journey

A sequential path from awareness to advocacy. Comparable to belt progression in martial arts — each stage deepens engagement and learning.

Continuous Improvement (Kaizen)

The practice of incremental refinement through small, consistent actions. A cornerstone of both Japanese martial training and modern brand management.

D

Discipline: The cornerstone of mastery. In the dojo, it's repetition; in marketing, it's consistent execution and follow-through. The invisible force behind excellence.

Dojo: A training hall or sacred learning space in martial arts. This book represents the marketer's space for disciplined practice — whether an office, agency, or creative lab.

Dojo Mindset: A philosophy of continuous learning, humility, and self-improvement. The belief that mastery is a journey, not an endpoint.

Duality: The coexistence of opposing forces — attack and defense, emotion and logic, short-term and long-term strategy. Recognizing and balancing dualities defines mastery.

E

Empathy: The ability to perceive another's thoughts and feelings — essential in both martial engagement and customer insight. Empathy transforms persuasion into understanding.

Ethical Branding: A marketing approach rooted in transparency, respect, and accountability. Reflects the Bushidō principle of acting with honor even under pressure.

Execution Discipline: The ability to transform ideas into consistent, measurable results. Mirrors the martial artist's repetition of fundamentals until perfection.

F

Flow (Mushin): A psychological state of total absorption and effortless action, described by Mihaly Csikszentmihalyi. In martial arts, it's mushin ("no-mind"); in marketing, it's creative immersion where intuition and analytics align.

Focus (Kime): In martial training, the concentration of energy at the point of impact. In marketing, the discipline to channel resources toward a single, resonant message or objective.

G

Growth Mindset: According to Carol Dweck, abilities can be developed through effort and learning. The marketer's version of the student's journey from white belt to black belt.

Grit: Angela Duckworth's term for sustained passion and perseverance. In martial arts, it's the willingness to get up after every fall; in marketing, it's resilience through failed campaigns and volatile markets.

H

Harmony: The blending of intention and context — the ability to resolve conflict without aggression. A key tenet in Aikido and in collaborative, customer-centric marketing.

Humility (Shoshin): The "beginner's mind" — staying open to learning regardless of experience. Prevents ego from halting growth. Essential for innovation and adaptation.

I

Integrity: The alignment between values and actions. In both martial and marketing disciplines, integrity creates trust — the invisible currency of mastery.

Iteration: The process of repeated testing and refinement. Equivalent to the martial artist's drills or kata, each round brings deeper precision.

J

Jeet Kune Do: Bruce Lee's hybrid martial art that emphasizes efficiency and adaptability. Symbolic of integrated marketing — using no fixed method, only what works.

Judo Principle (Leverage): Maximizing impact with minimal force. In marketing, it's turning small insights or budgets into outsized influence through timing and creativity.

K

Kaizen: Japanese principle meaning "continuous improvement." Adopted by Toyota and global business leaders, rooted in martial discipline and mindful repetition.

Kata: Formalized sequences of movement in martial arts — repeated drills that embody core techniques. In marketing, it represents structured practice routines that refine consistency and creativity.

Kime: Focus or decisive energy applied at a single moment. The art of striking with intention — whether in combat or communication.

L

Lineage: The unbroken transmission of knowledge from teacher to student. In marketing, this equates to mentorship and legacy — passing strategy, ethics, and culture through generations.

Loyalty: A long-term bond built on respect and reliability. In martial arts, loyalty to one's dojo; in marketing, loyalty between brand and consumer.

M

Mastery: The continuous pursuit of perfection through deliberate practice. A state where knowledge becomes instinct, and action becomes art.

Martial Metaphor: The use of combat and discipline imagery to illuminate strategic, ethical, and psychological parallels in marketing.

Mindfulness: Present-moment awareness. In both arts, it transforms reaction into response and chaos into clarity.

Mixed Martial Arts (MMA) of Marketing: The integration of diverse marketing disciplines — data analytics, storytelling, psychology, and design — into one fluid strategic system.

Mushin (No-Mind): The state of mental emptiness where thought and action merge. Enables peak creativity and responsiveness.

N

Narrative Resonance: When a brand story emotionally synchronizes with audience values — creating belonging rather than mere persuasion.

Neuroplasticity: The brain's ability to reorganize and adapt through learning. Explains how repetition and humility deepen mastery.

P

Perception (Zanshin): Seeing beyond the surface — sensing energy, tone, and timing. In marketing, the art of reading between data points and cultural signals.

Purpose: The "why" behind action. The martial artist's path (Do) and the marketer's mission both derive meaning from purpose rather than profit.

Positioning: Defining a unique and defendable space in the audience's mind. Parallels the martial concept of stance — strategic placement before movement.

Precision: Exactness in timing, technique, and tone. The essence of mastery in both strike and strategy.

R

Randori: Free sparring in martial arts — unscripted testing of skills under pressure. In marketing, it equates to live campaign testing and rapid adaptation.

Repetition: The foundation of instinctive skill. Each cycle of refinement — whether a kata or a campaign — carves neural pathways for precision.

Resilience: The ability to recover and grow from setbacks. Every failed strike or failed campaign strengthens future response.

Respect (Rei): The act of honoring teachers, peers, and opponents. The first and last gesture in martial arts — and the cornerstone of brand ethics.

S

Samurai Ethic: The moral foundation of the warrior: courage, loyalty, integrity, and honor. Its modern counterpart in business is servant leadership and brand accountability.

Sensei: Teacher or mentor. In marketing, the guiding strategist transfers wisdom, not just instruction.

Shoshin (Beginner's Mind): An attitude of openness and curiosity, even for experts. Encourages learning and prevents complacency.

Strategy (Heihō): The art of aligning tactics to long-term purpose. Derived from The Art of War and The Book of Five Rings.

T

Tactical Adaptation: The ability to respond in real-time to opponent or market movement — agility without loss of structure.

Timing (Maai): The distance and rhythm between opponents or events. In marketing, it refers to releasing messages when audience readiness peaks.

Trust: The invisible outcome of ethical conduct and consistent value. In both arts, trust is earned slowly and lost instantly.

U

UFC (Ultimate Fighting Championship): A modern example of branding through personality and narrative. Fighters embody archetypes that mirror classic brand storytelling.

Unconscious Competence: The final stage of mastery — performing flawlessly without conscious thought. The marketer's equivalent of creative instinct or brand intuition.

V

Value Creation: The essence of both disciplines — to contribute more than one extracts. The martial artist seeks peace; the marketer seeks purpose-driven impact.

Visualization: Mental rehearsal used by athletes, martial artists, and top marketers to preempt action with imagination.

W

White Belt Mindset: Approaching each challenge as a beginner, regardless of experience. The secret to perpetual relevance.

Winning (Shōri): Redefined as harmony rather than conquest. The best brands and fighters seek balance, not dominance.

Z

Zanshin: A term denoting ongoing awareness — readiness of mind and spirit even after the action ends. In marketing, it's the sustained attentiveness to audience response post-campaign.

Zen Strike: A term coined in this book to describe minimalist, decisive, and meaningful communication — where simplicity becomes impact.

Closing Note

In martial arts, words point to principles, but mastery comes from embodiment. This glossary serves as a bridge — translating the spirit of the dojo into the language of the market. Every term here is both metaphor and method: a reminder that strategy without soul is hollow, and that in both combat and communication, presence is the ultimate weapon.

Annotated Bibliography and Notes — Chapter-wise

Introduction — Why Compare Marketing and Martial Arts?

- Lee, Bruce. Tao of Jeet Kune Do. Ohara Publications, 1975.
- Establishes adaptability ("Be like water") as the philosophical core shared by martial arts and marketing.
- Kotler, Philip & Keller, Kevin Lane. Marketing Management, 16th ed., Pearson, 2022.
- Defines marketing as a system of value creation — the intellectual foundation for comparing it with mastery disciplines.
- Sun Tzu. The Art of War, trans. Lionel Giles, 1910.
- Source of strategic maxims on timing and positioning that parallel tactical marketing behavior.
- Csikszentmihalyi, Mihaly. Flow: The Psychology of Optimal Experience. Harper & Row, 1990.
- Connects martial immersion and creative flow in brand building.
- Gladwell, Malcolm. Outliers: The Story of Success. Little Brown, 2008.

The "10,000-hour rule" supports the book's argument that repetition and discipline underpin mastery in both arts.

Section 1 — Foundations

- Funakoshi, Gichin. Karate-Do: My Way of Life. Kodansha, 1975.

  Provides moral grounding — self-improvement over competition — analogous to purpose-driven marketing.
- Drucker, Peter. Management: Tasks, Responsibilities, Practices. Harper & Row, 1973.

  Reframes marketing as understanding the customer; parallels martial self-awareness.

- Holt, Douglas. How Brands Become Icons. Harvard Business Review Press, 2004.

  Historical basis for brands as cultural masters, not combatants.
- Heath, Chip & Heath, Dan. Made to Stick. Random House, 2007.

  Illustrates the simplicity principle — clarity through form, as in kata.

Section 2 — Core Similarities

- Ericsson, K. Anders et al. The Cambridge Handbook of Expertise and Expert Performance. Cambridge UP, 2006.

  Empirical model of deliberate practice underpinning mastery narratives.
- Dweck, Carol S. Mindset. Random House, 2006.

  A growth mindset is the dojo ethos of continuous learning.
- Duckworth, Angela. Grit. Scribner, 2016.

  Demonstrates perseverance as a stronger predictor of success than talent.
- Skinner, B. F. Science and Human Behavior. Free Press, 1953.

  Behavioral reinforcement theory informs repetitive training parallels.
- Bruce Lee Foundation Archives. Jeet Kune Do Notes and Letters.

Primary reflections on adaptability and anti-rigidity; conceptual base for marketing fluidity.

Section 3 — Key Differences

- Kahneman, Daniel. Thinking, Fast and Slow. FSG, 2011.

Framework for reflexive vs. deliberate thinking — physical vs. psychological engagement.

- Binet, Les & Field, Peter. The Long and the Short of It. IPA, 2013.

  Empirical anchor for tactical vs. strategic focus.
- MIT Human Dynamics Lab. "The Science of Teams." Harvard Business Review, Apr 2012.

  Team cohesion research linked to dojo collaboration models.
- Csikszentmihalyi & Nakamura. "The Concept of Flow." Oxford UP, 2002.

  Differentiates transient success from enduring presence.

Section 4 — Martial Arts Principles for Marketers

- Toyota Motor Corp. Kaizen Philosophy Docs, 1986.

Basis for "Marketing Kata" — structured improvement cycles.

- HBR. "The Power of Small Wins." May 2011.
  Data supporting incremental progress as a motivational engine.
- Lee, Bruce. The Warrior Within. McGraw-Hill, 1996.
  Source of "using no way as way" applied to creative flexibility.

Section 5 — Strategy and Tactics

- Taleb, Nassim Nicholas. Antifragile. Random House, 2012.
  Foundational text for resilience through stress.
- Sun Tzu. The Art of War, Chs IV & VI.
  Tactical timing and positioning concepts.
- HBR. "Adaptability: The New Competitive Advantage." Jul–Aug 2011.
  Corporate evidence for adaptive strategy.
- Netflix Case Archive, 2007–2012.
  Demonstrates pivot as a strategic flow application.

Section 6 — Values at the Core

- Ueshiba, Morihei. The Art of Peace. Shambhala, 1992.
  Ethics and non-aggression as brand philosophy.
- Patagonia. The Responsible Company. 2012.
  Case study of Bushidō-like corporate ethics.
- Suzuki, Shunryu. Zen Mind, Beginner's Mind. 1970.
  The concept of shoshin underpins humility and innovation.
- Unilever (Dove Campaign).
  Demonstrates ethical courage in challenging industry stereotypes.

Section 7 — Real-World Examples & Case Studies

- UFC Media Archives, 2018.
  Fighters as brands: identity and story architecture.
- Garage Beer, "Brewmite" Campaign, 2018.
  Martial narrative used to illustrate focus and craft.
- Spotify, "Wrapped," 2019-24.
  Adaptive personalization and emotional resonance.
- Nike, Just Do It Retrospective, 1988-2023.

Long-term discipline in message consistency.

- Apple, Patagonia, and Netflix Annual Reports.
  Long-view brand mastery and philosophical continuity.

Section 8 — Application Toolkit

- Toyota Production System (TPS).
  Iterative improvement model for "Marketing Kata."
- IDEO. Design Thinking Playbook, 2015.
  Creative synchrony and team flow.
- Google Re:Work, "Psychological Safety and Team Performance," 2015.
  Evidence for the flow state team framework.
- HubSpot Academy Curricula, 2018.
  Belt-progression learning path analogy.
- Ogilvy Archives, 1980-2020.
  Mentorship and creative lineage culture.

Section 9 — Pitfalls and Misconceptions

- McKinsey & Co. "The Multi-Skilled Marketer," 2022.
  Quantifies the value of cross-functional generalists.
- Haig, Matt. Brand Failures. Kogan Page, 2011.
  Ego and over-specialization as collapse drivers.
- Binet & Field. Marketing Effectiveness in the Digital Age, IPA, 2020.
  Activity ≠ impact — reinforces focus principle.
- UCL Neuroscience, "Attention Fatigue Studies," 2018.
  Scientific basis for strategic minimalism and restraint.

Section 10 — Conclusion — The Path to Mastery and Market Dominance

- Musashi, Miyamoto. The Book of Five Rings. Shambhala, 2012.
  Mastery as awareness; used as a final thesis anchor.
- Taleb, Nassim Nicholas. Antifragile. (Referenced again.)
  Closing the loop between discipline and resilience.
- Patagonia, Nike, Apple Reflections.
  Illustrations of harmony over dominance.

- Yamamoto, Tsunetomo. Hagakure: The Book of the Samurai. Kodansha, 1979.

  Ethical coda: service and humility as true strength.

General Notes

- Psychological frameworks (Flow, Grit, Mindset, Antifragility) anchor philosophical themes in empirical research.
- Martial texts and modern marketing theory are cross-referenced to demonstrate continuity between Do ("the Way") and professional practice.
- Corporate case studies (Nike, Dove, Patagonia, Netflix, Spotify, Apple) sourced from verifiable reports and archives.

Recurring motif — "discipline as freedom" — draws on neuroscience of habit formation (Duhigg, 2012).

Closing Reflection

These references trace a lineage of ideas from Bruce Lee to Kotler, from Musashi to Csikszentmihalyi.

Together they affirm that mastery is not a destination but a discipline — the intersection of awareness, repetition, and purpose.

Both the marketer and the martial artist seek the same state: clarity in motion, integrity in impact.

About the Author

Subba Rao Chaganti is a pioneering voice at the intersection of pharmaceutical marketing, behavioral science, and emerging technologies. With over three decades of industry experience and a prolific portfolio of over 30 groundbreaking books on pharmaceutical strategy, Chaganti is widely regarded as a thought leader who redefines how pharma educates, engages, and empowers.

He began his journey as a marketing educator and practitioner, driven by a singular mission: to bridge the gap between science and storytelling in pharma. Today, his work spans disciplines—from sales force effectiveness and key account management to digital therapeutics, wearable tech, internal branding, and AI-powered brand strategy.

Beyond the books, Chaganti is a mentor to brand managers, a respected voice on LinkedIn and Substack, and an unwavering advocate for ethical, patient-centered innovation in life sciences marketing. His ability to translate complexity into actionable strategy makes his work not just readable—but indispensable.

He lives in Farmington, Connecticut, USA, and can be reached at: subbarao.chaganti@gmail.com.

Here is a list of his publications:

1. Pharmaceutical Marketing in India: Concepts, Cases, Strategy
2. Game Plans for Post-GATT Era: Action Agenda of the Indian Pharmaceutical Industry
3. Compete or Forfeit: Strategies for Sustainable Competitive Advantage in the Pharma Product Patents Era
4. Pharmaceutical Marketing in India for Today and Tomorrow - 25th Anniversary Edition
5. Bullseyes and Blunders: Lessons from 100 Cases in Pharma Marketing

6. Digital Pharma Marketing Playbook: Winning With the New Rules of Engagement
7. Cracking the Generics Code: Your Single-Source Success Manual for Winning in Multi-Source Product Markets
8. Reimagine Pharma Marketing: Make It Future-Proof!
9. Brand Positioning in Pharma
10. Transactional to Transformational Marketing in Pharma: The Science of Why and The Art of How
11. A to Z of Pharmaceutical Marketing: World's First and Only Encyclopedia in Two Volumes
12. The Synergy of Minds: Human+AI Orchestrating the Pharma Marketing Revolution
13. Design Thinking for Pharma
14. The Pharma Product Manager: Navigating the Digital Frontier
15. Sentiment Analysis for Pharma Marketers
16. Whispering to AI: Prompt Engineering for Pharma Brand Managers
17. Storytelling in Pharma Marketing
18. Beyond the Molecule: The Art and Science of Metaphors That Matter
19. The Voices Within: Your Body Speaks, When your organs tell their own stories
20. Pharma Archetypes: The Science of Meaningful Healthcare Marketing
21. Navigating the AI Revolution: Human Futures
22. Breaking Through: A Business Novel (based on the theory of constraints)
23. Code to Cure: Digital Therapeutics and the Future of Pharma
24. The Wearable Edge: Redefining Pharma Marketing in a Connected and Data-Driven World
25. Tarun Gupta: The Man who taught Marketing to the Indian Pharmaceutical Industry
26. The Inner Game of Marketing: Mastering the Mind Behind the Message
27. Level Up: Gamification in Pharma Marketing
28. Marketing Fundamentals.
29. The Digital Marketer's Playbook: Strategies, Frameworks, and Tools for the New Marketing Era
30. Advertising in the Age of Generative AI: How Agencies, Creatives, and Brands Win

31. The Good Pharma: Remembering the Medicines, Discoveries, and People Who Changed Human Life
32. Key Account Management: Strategies for Success

www.ingramcontent.com/pod-product-compliance
Lightning Source LLC
Chambersburg PA
CBHW071224230926
51849CB00001B/22